Protests of an Ex-Organization Man

Protests

OF AN

EX-ORGANIZATION

MAN

By KERMIT EBY

BEACON PRESS   BOSTON

This book is based on articles by the author which have
appeared in the following periodicals: *American Journal of
Economics and Sociology, Antioch Review, Brethren Life
and Thought, Bulletin of American Colleges, Christian
Century, Christian Scholar, Journal of Political Science,
Journal of Sociology, Progressive, Religion and Life.*

The author wishes to acknowledge with thanks
the assistance of Don Tonjes in research and
preparation of the footnotes.

To Retha, who held the home base

Contents

Preface ix
1. A Confession of Bias 1
2. Men—Not Monuments 8
3. Let Your Yea Be Yea 16
4. Education for Sectarians 22
5. Like unto Our Heroes 27
6. The Cruelest Decision 33
7. Why Labor Leaders Are Lonesome 39
8. On Workers' Education 46
9. Organization, Bureaucracy, Loyalty 49
10. Democracy through Decision 56
11. Labor and Political Action 64
12. Becoming an Organization Man 73
13. Kept Men 82
14. Study Them Alive 87
15. The Wirepullers 96
16. Never the Twain Shall Meet 106
17. The Moral Dilemma of Democratic Man . . . 113
18. Peace, Politics and Pragmatism 122
19. Labor, Politics and Protestantism 129
    Epilogue: Invocation for a Meeting of Brethren Ministers 137
    Index 141

Preface

This book is about struggles and changes in organized labor, education and religion. My opinions have been shaped by six years as an employee with the Chicago Teachers Union and six more with the national CIO. The essays in this book have the look and feel of those efforts—the labor movement, the religious activities and the educational whirl—which I have touched.

I was born on September 21, 1903 in St. Joseph County, Indiana. My ancestors on both sides were Anabaptist-Pietists, Mennonites and Brethren. The Ebys were birthright Mennonites. One of my ancestors, seven generations removed, was a Mennonite bishop, Christian Eby. The Schwalms, my mother's people, were Brethren. My father and mother grew up on practically adjoining farms. They married young, and I was their first child. I would be Mennonite today if my Grandfather Schwalm, a Brethren elder, hadn't refused to permit his daughter "to be unequally yoked with unbelievers." So my father was baptized a Brethren. When I was about ten we moved from my Grandfather Eby's farm (Mennonite) to one Dad bought from Grandfather Schwalm (Brethren). From then on my world was increasingly Brethren. Every intellectual and spiritual problem of my life springs from this heritage. To this day I am busy trying to reconcile the face-to-face ethic of my youth with the problems of our age.

The Mennonites and Brethren are peace churches. Historically they were pacifist and withdrawing. My radicalism evolves from this heritage. My pre-World War II experiences as a "plain" boy, conscious of my German descent and seeing our church painted "yellow," made a deep impression on me. So, I early became interested in peace.

Determined to understand my heritage, I broke with the farm, worked in a factory and on construction gangs, taught all eight elementary grades, and put myself through Manchester College, one of our church schools. Here I went out to the churches to teach peace to pacifists.

The more I went to school, the greater was my hunger for answers. I taught, preached and, with my wife's help, saved for graduate education. From 1929 to 1931, I studied international relations at the University of Chicago. Here I was told repeatedly that my professors could make a scholar out of me if I but gave up wanting to remake the world. It was at Chicago that I was converted to democratic socialism.

In 1931, I went to teach at Ann Arbor High School, because it paid more than any college job. This was one of those chances which determine a life. Ann Arbor was Michigan, and Michigan became the laboratory for CIO organization.

In 1933 my teaching was gloriously interrupted by a six-month peace mission to the Orient. There I felt very much in touch with history, and very much a part of it. I came home more militant than ever.

I became an organizer for the Teachers Union and a member of the Michigan Socialist Party, where I met Walter Reuther. I helped the automobile workers organize and participated in the sit-down strikes. In 1936, I was suspended and tried for corrupting the youth of Ann Arbor; in the trial the students and community supported me.

In 1937, I left teaching to become executive secretary of the Chicago Teachers Union. From 1937 to 1941, I fought the Kelly-Nash political machine and union apathy. In 1941, I was fired for insubordination.

Early in 1942, I went to the CIO in Washington as First Assistant Director of Research and Education. In 1945, I succeeded Raymond Walsh as Director.

Most of my time was spent lobbying and petitioning the government, but I found time to represent the CIO at UNESCO and at MacArthur's Commission for the Reorganization of Education in Japan.

I came to the University of Chicago in 1948, a Hutchins man and appointee. Here I teach the life and loves of Kermit Eby, under such titles as Social Science and the Value Problem. In addition, I write a bit, circuit-ride, garden and spoil my grandchildren.

Outwardly, I may appear urbane; inwardly, I remain a Brethren-Mennonite farm boy, trying to reconcile his worlds.

The six years in the Ann Arbor school system taught me that a teacher could propagandize his students in support of the Republican party, a so-called free enterprise economy and something called individual initiative, but woe to the teacher who supported the Democratic party, interested himself in organized labor and worked for a cooperative society. Through such experiences I learned early that the greatest evils grow out of silence. The minds of our youth are colored as much by what we do not teach as by what we do.

I am aware that most alert readers will easily discover my bias—that of the analyst who writes from experience rather than from cold and considered scholarship. However, so that there be no doubts about my biases, I should like to state briefly my stand on the various issues under discussion.

First, I believe that real political education requires the thorough teaching of hard facts about political parties and their financial needs. I believe that parents and teachers have over-emphasized the importance of bringing up our sons as future Presidents and have neglected the importance of teaching them to be precinct captains.

Second, I believe that there is too great a tendency on the part of educators to gloss over the ills of our acquisitive society. Something is amiss when labor's children are hostile to the aims of organized labor. Too long, school boards have been filled with business and professional men who have little concern for the interests of any population group outside of their own. The time has come for organized labor to vote its representatives onto boards of education. The time has also come to examine curricula and textbooks to find out why so little emphasis is given to labor's contribution to democracy, why cooperatives are ignored in history and civics courses and why social legislation is so often taught as a necessary evil.

Third, as a believer in the potentiality of a cooperative society, I must directly challenge our present acquisitive society. I believe that labor, which once challenged acquisitive society, has come more and more to make its peace with a "mixed economy." We who continue to challenge our acquisitive society declare to the world our conviction that the profit motive is not divine inspiration, and that service is as powerful a motive as ownership for getting things done. Capitalism, as I define it, is that form of economic organization built on the profit motive. It is the kind of legal and business system in which almost everyone works for wages and only a handful of people owns and controls the mines, factories and railroads. These few owners also indirectly control the schools, with the results I have mentioned.

There are other results. The majority of the managers and professional men of America are happy in their work. The majority of industrial workers are dissatisfied. They tell me that they feel enslaved to the machine, that they desire the status which only recognition of their creativity can give. Today they are bribed by full employment to endure their unhappiness; but given a situation in which several millions are again unemployed, resentment may reach a climax making it possible for the totalitarians of right or left to come into their own.

That is why it is our responsibility to examine the nature of our industrial society, accept unions as equally sovereign with management, encourage workers' education, organize our corporations to make the workers partners in production and arrange that, when productivity increases, the benefits go into wages as well as profits. Above all, we must build direct channels of communication between workers and management; we must create situations in which men meet as equals and in which power with, not power over, guides discussion. The formation of a democratically organized industry is a challenge to all of us. Workers are not interested in abstractions. They want democracy, economic as well as political, to play a part in daily life.

Fourth, I believe that economic and political democracy will be impossible for Americans until there are enough of us whose outlook is world-wide. Since the hydrogen bomb, there is no longer any security for us except within the framework of an organized and peaceful world. This means the limitation of sovereignty, the substitution of international loyalties for nationalism, and disarmament. The predatory and imperialistic activities of capitalism and of imperialistic communism must be curbed.

And I have a bias toward education with an emphasis on content rather than gadgets. Especially we who are interested in workers' education should learn to relate what we teach in the present to man's continuous struggle throughout the ages for a better world. We must be determined to draw upon the present experience of our people, for conditions found in present experience give meaning where mere abstractions fail; and workers, conscious of their own struggle for a better life, are apt to be sympathetic with workers everywhere.

In other words, I stand with many unionists and educators in believing that ideals are practical. I, like them, reject the thesis that only the selfish individualist can be trusted to reconstruct the world. In fact, we argue that the idealists could not possibly do a worse job of reconstruction than is being done by the hard-bitten men called "realists."

It is imperative, then, that both workers' education and general education emphasize the kind of learning which will strengthen and broaden character, develop discrimination and help men to form sound judgments. Education—if it be called education at all—must seek the truth, free from dogma and doctrinaire instruction. Men and women who desire to be effective and useful in education must have a point of view, a method of approach to their problems and a respect for facts. They must be able to dig out relevant facts, to face them after they have dug them out and to generalize on the basis of what they have discovered. Intellectual integrity, not prejudice, should be the goal of education. But even more, the real success of a teacher depends on how well he relates the new experiences of his students to their backgrounds. Teachers who cannot understand the lives and backgrounds of their students, who do not live, who are not active citizens, can never be really great teachers.

1. A Confession of Bias

I am a partisan. I not only admit this fact, I am proud of it. For me, partisanship has something to do with being a sectarian and even more to do with being a protestant with the accent on the penult: pro-test-ant—one who asserts, and one who objects.

I come by some of this quite naturally. My people were Brethren Protestants. They were also sectarian in the old-fashioned sense—worshiping narrow and exact gods. These gods discriminated between one act and another quite precisely; the acts they omitted were simply nonexistent in the Brethren world. Since the Brethren who brought me up were Indiana farm folk, a great many subtle moral problems which are indigenous to any urban intelligentsia were beyond their comprehension. They were a sturdy people, those by whom America, in fable and story, was built.

These Brethren excluded as dangerous and sinful the actions which they found most tempting. Their temptations were the basic ones: worship of false ideals of character like the proud overworked and the successful acquisitive, indulgence in satisfying but hurtful gossip, undisciplined yielding to emotions, and loss of faith. Since the Brethren were truly sectarian, they took issue with the larger body of Protestantism. Special laws were made against the sordid but gratifying wars, and this resulted in one of their official doctrines, pacifism.

In my youth, the Brethren were unswervingly Republican. They *identified*, as the sophisticated phrase goes, with the Republicans because the Republicans were reputed to be hard-working, solvent and churchgoing. The image of the Democrat was that of a flighty man, inclined to live on credit and even occasionally engaged in freethinking. It was impossible to tell about the Democrats' sex life, but the Brethren had their suspicions.

I grew up in an era when political slogans were simple and straight to the point. For example:

Hurrah for Teddy
He's the man.
If I can't vote,
My Daddy can!

Like many sons of ultraconservative parents, I rebelled. I went Democrat and Labor New Deal in the thirties. I even became an official of the national CIO. I associated with women who believed in free love, and with men who believed in free trade, freethinking and free meals for the destitute. I knew men who lived hard, drank hard, played hard, never saved money, men who were part and parcel of the striving, corrupt world, and died in most cases of heart attacks. It was precisely this splaying of intention, this dissoluteness of effect, that my people had tried to protect me against.

It was in those days that T. S. Eliot took to monarchy in politics, Anglicanism in religion and classicism in poetry. Fitzgerald took to Europe and came back trying to save his money and his health. Hemingway, meanwhile, took to that satisfying and strangely meaningful Civil War in Spain. And people of all kinds took to vitamin pills and abstraction, existentialism and hyper-respectability, theories on art and theories on love, Stalinism and nudism.

I took to the same old church in disguise. The Sectarians of the Left—the Schachmanites, Trotskyites, Lovestoneites, Socialists, Social Democrats, Social Fascists—all, somehow, were disturbingly similar to the faces from my youth. I had seen the same expressions on the inflamed and ecstatic face of the local parson preaching against sin, drink, bad women and bad money.

A sectarian is recognizable anywhere. He refuses to worship all or any gods except his own; his religion is narrow, dialectical and arbitrarily intense. The true sectarian is biased, and willing to work himself, his wife, his children, his favorite dog and his most faithful horse to the bone in the name of his bias. That bias represents his idea of how the world should, ideally, be. If he is a spiritualist, it is an eternal world; if he is a humanist, it is a world based on the eternity of children: for our children or the children of our comrades, we gladly give the blood of this generation. I do not know that I like or commend this image, but I do know that I am part of it. I do not know that I like or am at peace with that always protesting Protestant Brethren heritage, but I know that it is a part of me.

My conscience presented all sorts of problems when I came to the University of Chicago. If this were the home of the objective, the brave and the true, I had no other choice but to confess my bias at the beginning of each course. I believe that a man can only teach well when he feels deeply, and when a man feels deeply, he is most often given to dramatization. Drama is very much part of effective teaching. Thus, my classes are biased by my own view—my philosophy, if you prefer—as well as by my own method: parables and a reliving of what I had experienced.

Another part of my bias-orientation is personal contact with my students. Theories are connected with human personalities, with subjectivity. Consequently, I leave my door open to students; whatever I have to say as a sectarian is often most effectively said as a personality.

This is not meant to disparage my scholarly colleagues in any way. When I came to the University of Chicago, I found that many members of the staff refused to keep their doors open. Some of them were sincere in the gesture of the closed door; they wanted to read, to study, to observe, to write and, in the end, to reveal to a small, discriminating world the results of their study, observations and reading. What they want to find is not to be sought in the heedless, moment-to-moment world. For these men I have the greatest respect. They are sectarian in the purest sense; they share that pure-souled belief in otherworldliness which my own Protestant heritage failed to achieve because it was too near the demanding, shrill needs of the earth.

There are others who close their doors for whom I do not have that respect. These are the intelligentsia whom you can see any day in the drawing rooms selling out their right to protest, to encourage other human beings and to exchange honest ideas in honest fashion with other workmen of their trade. These are the teachers who start each day with a good word of the current gobbledygook to the head of the department. These are the teachers who do not close their doors to students because they need privacy and quiet to see better. No matter what they try to see, their vision is clogged by ambition. Rather be the most narrow, even bigoted, sectarian than a man who blows neither hot nor cold except at the discretion of the department head; who invariably pursues the current line. "A murderer is 'disturbed'; let us discuss how he is disturbed." But we do not really discuss it. We only repeat some sociological gobbledygook. We dare not admit that we understand. We dare not admit our common basic humanity. It is this attempt to deny the often disturbing roots of humanhood that lies behind the protests of many social scientists to unyielding objectivity.

One woman, a fledgling in the social science field, with whom I was attempting to have a conversation concerning the primitive, animal bases of all humanhood, belonged to the "all is conditioning" school. I was trying to point out that just under the skin of civilized man lie primitive lusts of great savagery and great goodness. It was her contention that she and her kind were so well civilized that under no condition would they ever commit murder, mayhem or any of the other crimes of lust. As she was saying these things, however, her face swelled with the animal fury of verbal combat. In the end she was shouting at me that her passions had been toned down to nothing by the socialization process.

It seems to me that those who study man should be more imaginative than endlessly to count noses of dissent. The rage among statisticians for proving or disproving things by means of numbers seems to have caught hold of the entire social science field. It is part of the passion for objectivity, a passion which I suspect in the same way that I suspected the lady who cried out so loudly that she would never murder. Many of the sociologists I have known have been troubled men; they had been hurt by an insanely arbitrary disorder in human life. Sensitive men are offended by the senseless wars, the proclivity of people to hurt and hate one another, to divide each other into inferior and superior species according to some irrelevant factors of ethnic or social origin. This is one of the reasons why much of sociology today is concentrated on what is coyly called race relations. I suspect that enough sociologists are so pained by the festering state of race relations in the United States that they are willing to sell their souls to an IBM machine, if only the IBM will figure out some order from the senseless chaos. Those men with the strongest passions—ambition, love, hate, avarice, generosity—are often the most passionate in camouflaging their feelings and trying to find a scientific explanation for them.

Many of these passionate objectivists strike me as deeply sectarian. They are passionately dispassionate. Life—subjective, horrifying, brilliantly colored, amazing, intense—flows on all about them, yet like my Brethren ancestors, who sent the Church after Life and told it to behave itself, these social scientists expect to keep life under control with a hygienic set of index cards.

My quarrel is not with the principle: the human race has always had a job in attempting to control or channel its emotions. To create order out of chaos is certainly the job of thoughtful human beings, among whom can be numbered quite a few social scientists. But what kind of order—and order for what?

I suppose the real question, buried at the core of any discussion of this kind, is the nature of bias itself. Bias in the deepest sense goes beyond reason and beyond politics. A man may spend his whole life (with or without the cost of a thorough psychoanalysis) discovering his true bias: the way he must go, the people he desires to be with, the things he has to do. If a man goes against his real bias too long and too fervently, if he pretends too competently to be something that he is not, he is apt to run into real trouble.

An old acquaintance of mine exemplifies this. John J. had been in my classroom and in the classrooms of my colleagues at the university. As a student he was bright, willing to work, normally

idealistic and normally willful. He had ideas, and he was verbal—
a not uncommon University of Chicago type. After graduate school
he became a teacher—at four thousand a year. He had a wife and
children; but four thousand didn't stretch, as his limply hanging
clothes indicated. He needed new clothes, and his wife needed a
new washing machine. Finally he gave in and joined an advertising agency—at eight thousand a year.

I visited him recently. He was angry with me at the time. He
had asked me for candidates for a job in his agency, and I had sent
him a woman who was bright, good-looking, sensitive and Negro.
He seemed to blame me for the fact that she was Negro. He called
me unrealistic. I reminded him that he had not mentioned the
color of skin required for the job; he had only specified the sort of
intelligence he wanted. I hated to tell him the obvious thing—that
he was the person who was unrealistic, and that not to deal with
Negroes as economic and job equals was inimical to his own business in these United States.

Our conversation continued, however, and he told me how
happy the agency had made him. He said that when he went
home to Hyde Park, where he lived, he could have dinner with
anybody he wanted to, Negro, Jew, even Anglo-Saxon. But he
would never, of course, have lunch with a Negro friend uptown in
the Loop area unless it happened to be Ralph Bunche or Marian
Anderson. At the climax of this discussion, he brought out his ulcer
pills to prove to me that he was a real honest-to-God advertising
man, now making fifteen or eighteen thousand dollars a year.

This proof that one part of John J.'s guts was at war with the
other part convinced me that he was getting far too little for all the
work he had to do. If a man doesn't stick with his bias, he is apt to
land in trouble: sudden paralysis of the liver, the heart, the spleen
or the right hand that does the work with the ink. Whatever his
bias, a man ought to get back to it before it is too late, before his
hand begins to shake or a tic develops because one part of him is
fighting against another.

I hope I have made my own bias clear. Before I was old
enough to choose, I was given a religion. Later, I found my own

religion in the social sense, and I sang in earnest all the old union and radical songs which are now reserved for the museums or the singers of quaint, archaic folksongs. I liked CIO in its a-birthing stage, and one of the reasons I liked it is that I am biased toward those people in whom the blood runs high. The blood ran high in the youthful CIO in 1937.

One of the first meetings was held in the back of my car, which we had parked in an empty lot. In those days we were afraid to meet in the homes of the workers, who were being terrorized by Harry Bennett's hoodlums. There were five of us in the car: two workers, a social case worker, an old German scissors-grinder who read books and ground scissors, and myself. I talked to them about organizing. They were convinced, and they began to talk to their neighbors. The next time, eleven of us met, in an abandoned schoolhouse. The arguments we had originally worked out were repeated a thousand times in those few brief years of glorious growth. The reverberations of those years still echo in the south and in other areas where the movement has not yet been corrupted by respectability. But the flames which once struck upward no longer burn in a steady thrust. From time to time, like shooting stars, they burn brightly and then disappear.

Integrity, I suppose, is sticking to your original bias and seeing it through, or finding your real bias and facing it. I am for integrity, if only because life is very short and truth is hard to come by. There is no time for the obvious and elaborate subterfuges played by men who think they know better. If we are after truth, let us not obscure it with false images, false gods and flattering likenesses.

2. Men—Not Monuments

I have taught all age levels for a total of twenty-two years. I also spent twelve years in organized labor, and I have been a minister since 1927. This is my twelfth year at the University of Chicago, four years longer than I ever stayed put before. Occasionally I still feel surprised to find myself a professor at a university which Robert Hutchins once described as, "not a good university, simply the best." In less humble moments, however, I sometimes think my experience outside the academic world gives me standards of judgment which the purely academic man does not have.

For example, I once thought all Ph.D.'s were definitely brilliant—intellectual luminaries in the dark skies of mental mediocrity. Now I think that the Ph.D. is more often than not a mark of persistence, not unrelated to the ability of students to give their professors what the professors want. Perhaps this is a part of the vocationalism which makes a Ph.D. so necessary for those who aspire to college and university teaching. Therefore, recognizing this to be true, I sometimes encourage my students to earn their degrees as quickly and painlessly as possible, and then go about getting their education. In my more cynical moments I compare a Ph.D. to a card in Kenin's union (musicians) and remark, "Membership doesn't mean greater ability to play the flute, only more opportunities."

Specialization is quickly becoming the badge of a higher education, and I do not believe in specialization. My bias is in favor of a liberal education in the humanities and social sciences, which demands that each individual develop his own intellectual synthesis. The educated man, I am convinced, is he who can select from the welter of conflicting philosophies one which is to him reasonable and true, and then defend it.

Furthermore, when I was in the field of labor organization, I preferred individuals who were not overly specialized. Given a knowledge of sources, the ability to organize knowledge and the rarest of all qualities—the ability to exercise judgment—the individual can be specialized on the job. Actually, I found it comparatively easy to find a Ph.D. who could count the milk bottles in Alequippa, Pennsylvania and correlate them with milk consumption. The jobs that were hard to fill were those which demanded more imaginative qualities. For example, good pamphleteers were almost impossible to find, because pamphleteering demands concise integration of ideas, facility in expression, plus commitment.

Universities and colleges produce more "bricklayers" than writers. Papers and theses are built by taking one fact from one book, another from a second, still another from a third and then reassembling them. When I find an exciting, creative writer, I am tempted to keep him locked up as a natural resource. Pamphleteering demands conviction—a willingness to take a position and defend it. Of course, the convinced cannot make objectivity an absolute. Nor—and I am convinced of this—can any honest man. Though empiricism in the social sciences demands detachment, the statisticians increasingly corrupt the study of man. To worshipers at the altar of science, in more and more professions, truth becomes a matter of evidence, not emotion. My bias is of course the opposite. Man is more, much more, than a decimal point; and subjective, indeed intuitive, truth is also valid. For example, I would ask my students to read mobility studies, and sample voting behavior; but I would insist they read Stendhal's *The Red and the Black* and Lincoln Steffens' *Autobiography*. And if they had more than one course with me, I would ask them to ride streetcars and study man in his natural habitat.

I begin every teaching semester with a lecture called "A Confession of Bias." I then state my bias and ask any student who wishes to leave to feel free to do so. A few have! This is my understanding of "letting your yea be yea and your nay be nay." Because I believe in my own freedom to express my opinions, I try to develop students who are willing to express theirs. Therefore, I insist on knowing each student. My attitude is simple, and clearly stated: "A student is more important than a footnote." Believing this, my office door is always open. I have developed a personal rapport with almost all of my students. With many I am on a first name basis. Status and titles do not impress me, for I am convinced that a respect based on degrees and titles is shallow indeed. This is the reason I am so troubled by the emphasis on externals that now prevails in modern Brethren and other former fellowship circles. In the clearest possible language, I prefer Kermit Eby, man, to Kermit Eby, symbol—always recognizing, I might add, how important symbols are to those so dependent on externals.

Furthermore, I ask my students not to review a book but to compose a conversation with the author. And what trouble so many of them have! To them the written word is truth, something to be accepted, not to be argued with; and this is doubly so when the works become classics. My task, therefore, is cut out for me: I must instill a healthy irreverence in all those who believe that what is in print must necessarily be the truth. More than once students have asked me if I am trying to trick them into making a mistake. They simply do not believe I want them to be intellectually free. Or, as they tell me, even here at Chicago, conformity, not individualism, is rewarded. By the end of the quarter, however, most of them are convinced.

Instead of giving written exams, I ask each student to come to my office or home for an hour-and-a-half-long conversation. Of course, this takes energy and, as I get older, more than I sometimes have. But my wife insists if I am doing God's work, He will supply the energy.

In a sense I have come full cycle. I began in a world of the face-to-face ethic and am ending the same way. During the twenty-five-year interval, mine was the world of pamphlet and committee. But before someone too hastily assumes that I have abandoned organizational responsibility, I must assert that my chief intellectual preoccupation is determining how to give meaning to the Judaeo-Christian ethic, a face-to-face ethic, and one which nurtured me in face-to-face relationships in a world which has become so complex that decision is ever further removed.

In the world of politics and power I affirm *man,* insisting that it is not that I am so good but that some are so awful! But enough of this. I am only doing what I believe to be the greatest necessity of our era—affirming *man*—protesting, and protesting forever, that man, imaginative and creative, is more important than any system.

Actually, there are times when I think system is fast becoming one of man's most effective enemies. Let me illustrate with examples from my experience as a circuit rider in the ranks of the ministry. Time and again, probably because I am outside the bureaucratic structure and have a bit of a reputation for intellectual nonconformity, ministers pour out their doubts to me:

> I so wanted to be a prophet! The ministry was once a calling, a dedication, and now it has become a routine. Housekeeping takes all my time. I am forever involved in teas and budgets. I haven't time to read or study. My sermons are uninspired. In order to get along, to support my hostages to fortune, I must conform.

And yet another:

> Why, oh why, is it so much easier to get a big pile of masonry built than a staff to operate it? Air conditioners instead of educational directors; kitchens nicely furnished instead of competent secretaries; *monuments* instead of *men.*

And what I have heard said about bishops and headquarters would be heresy if repeated.

Resentment smolders against the everlasting superimposition of special days and special materials. "When, oh, when," one minister said, "will there be a Sunday all my own?" To all of these my reply is that

> *men* are more important than *monuments,* and if you believe it, you must affirm your belief by behaving as if you did, even though you cease being a good organizational man. The first step

in recapturing your freedom is to be willing to behave as if losing your security made no difference.

Perhaps the time has arrived to assert that all men who wish to be free to speak their minds should know how to use their hands. Why shouldn't intellectuals learn a trade? And perhaps our Brethren-Mennonite farmer-ministers, whose living was independent of their brethren, had an advantage in that their bread and butter was not threatened! I am sure that the rabbis of earlier times, who worked as they taught, were freer men than their modern descendants; their parables were certainly more relevant. It is not an accident that the most charismatic ministers in America are to be found in Negro pulpits. I am convinced that the farmer-ministers of fifty years ago preached more relevant sermons than are preached today by seminary-trained theologians.

Our churches parade the statistics of an ever-expanding membership; our schools are proud of their growing numbers of graduates; our unions boast of their dues-paying members. Too many of us assume that it is quantity, not quality that matters. The fallacy in such reasoning is simple, for the man is always more important than the system. Recently I checked through an officers' report of the AFL Teachers Union (published in *The American Teacher,* September 1956). The entire issue was devoted to salaries, tenure, retirements and other practical matters. These things are certainly important. But it seems to me that the real problems of teaching are created by a public school system in which teachers must keep endless records, teach heavy class loads, take on so-called extracurricular activities and in general act as father, counselor, official administrator, policeman, bookkeeper and politician.

Why not let the teacher concentrate on teaching, and give the PTA jobs, the hall monitorships, the bookkeeping and all the other time-consuming tasks to professional secretaries and policemen? Not only do we harry our teachers with a multitude of chores, we insist on harrying them further with loyalty oaths and taboos. I understand what Jesus meant when he said, "Seek ye first the Kingdom of God and his righteousness, and all these things shall be added unto you."

I am insisting upon a reaffirmation that the ultimate loyalties of every minister, teacher and labor leader must be to commitment, not to system. I have always found it easier to work for organizations when my loyalty was to a vision of the kingdom, and not to men in a power structure. Without loyalty to a vision, religion becomes religiosity and secularism transcends dedication.

When loyalty to a vision departs the labor movement, the union ceases to be a movement and gain replaces service as the dominant motive. And the desire for gain produces more monuments than men. In Washington, D.C., union halls are being dedicated every day, each more ostentatious than the last. As a cynical unionist once expressed it: "Nothing is too good for the workers —the workers the workers employ." But though the workers resent their officials' expenditures, they are also proud of the glass-topped desks their bosses enjoy. These union monuments are not fully equipped without bars and slot machines. One of my young proteges discovered that earnings from these "one-armed bandits" had financed his education. This discovery upset him, since he was idealistic and believed that economic choices are moral choices, that one's life is shaped by how one's money is earned.

The union movement would be served better if there were fewer Philip Murray and William Green Halls, and more Philip Murray and William Green Scholarships for the sons and daughters of working men. More full-support scholarships would enable many capable young people to have an advanced education, young people who would otherwise never see the inside of a college classroom. We could better serve the freedoms we talk about so much by providing scholarships than we could by holding our hands out to the government for educational subsidies that in fact provide for military training and research.

All that I have so far written here is expressed in my belief that ultimate moral choices are personal. I could write a book explaining the social conditions which produced Dave Beck, insisting, as I do, that he is a true product of the business mores of his times. Nevertheless, he is guilty of theft, and doubly guilty, because unions are service institutions, not business institutions. Nor are churches precisely community centers, or physical education plants or even kitchens. They are religious institutions dedicated to answering the important questions of man's nature and destiny.

I am, therefore, not only affirming *man,* but a particular kind of man, an inner-directed man, a man with a built-in plumb line, one who is conscious of the necessities of compromise, but who is also wise enough to understand that a man who is a man at all must at some time stand beyond compromise, beyond history. Here is the point where education is as much of the heart as of the head.

For those who wish to have a clearer picture of what I mean, I would suggest reading the history of the American soldiers who defected to the Communists in Korea, as reported in the *New Yorker.* If there is any moral in the story, it is that many of these were men who felt no responsibility to their fellow man, because they had no clear image of what being a man meant. To me, this is stark tragedy, for I am interested in the heroic, in man who transcends even what is expected of him. Perhaps this is why I am forever asking who our cultural heroes are and what dragons they fight. Or, to put it in other words, the Bible is a great book because its concerns are all noble concerns and its heroes are worth emulating. If I had my way, every child would have as many pictures of his heroes as I was fortunate enough to acquire. I am convinced that it was because of my concept of the heroic that four times in my life I was able to stand against system and affirm *man.* Twice I determined that to deny me the right to speak as I believed was to violate me, and twice I stood with man against the institutions that would violate him. The ultimate travesty is the insistence by those who place system first, that a single man can be sacrificed for the good of history. It is only men who laugh, men who cry, men who are hurt, men who bleed.

And so I will go on, ever affirming *man,* insisting as a teacher that students should be inviolable, that workers are not the rank and file, that church members are not statistics and that it is my job to inspire and then get out of the way—recognizing that if students and workers fail, it is as much my failure as theirs. And I must always remember that I cannot excite unless I am excited, or ask others to believe if I am unwilling to believe.

As a preacher I would go even further. I would bring the good news to anyone who would listen. A new believer would always receive priority over a new church. And of course I would go to those without a shepherd; I would not expect them to come to me. All this I would do because I believe in the incarnation, the word becoming flesh.

Candidly, it is because I believe in man that I am happy when my students say they will remember me longer than they will remember what I taught. In this there is a great glory and also great risk. For I must always remember that it is my task to free, not dominate. It is because I am capable of loving that I must also be capable of setting free. In a sense, I must both attract and repel at the same time, just as parents, sooner or later, must learn that to get their children back they must give them up. Only those who are willing to give up can be trusted to have.

This, then, is my conclusion. I affirm *man*. In so doing I affirm students not footnotes, believers not buildings. Man is not a statistic. While men are not equal in strength or talent, they are forever equal in essence, for they all bear the same dignity by the very nature of their creation.

3. Let Your Yea Be Yea

There are many traditions common to my Mennonite-Brethren ancestors which grow increasingly meaningful to me as time passes and my contacts with the world become more varied. One is their emphasis on integrity, another their refusal of the oath. These two positions are not unrelated.

It was a truism in the world in which I grew up—Elkhart, northern Indiana, forty years ago—that a good Brethren would never sign a note or swear to tell the truth. Both of these acts were regarded as a violation of his dignity as a man, justifying an inference of lack of integrity. So far as I know, my Grandfather Schwalm and his peers in the Baugo church were never guilty of either offense. As a result, I grew up with the boast, "A Dunkard's word is as good as his bond." As a boy, I realized that there was something unique in being so labeled. As a man with years of organizational experience in politics, labor, education—yes, even in church circles—I consciously realized its consequences.

Perhaps the Brethren position can best be described through illustrations. My Grandfather Schwalm, elder of the Church of the Brethren in our Baugo congregation, was a good friend of Jeremiah Bechtal, the banker in the town of Wakarusa. In those days, fifty years ago, when a young man wanted to "start up" farming, he usually had about $250 saved; to get a team, a few cows, chickens and tools, he would need $500 more. If this young man were a Dunkard or a neighbor of Grandfather's, Bechtal would ask Grandfather for a character affirmation. If Grandfather approved, the money was advanced, a notation made on the books, "Approved by Monroe Schwalm." And that was it! (May I hasten to add that such is not the case in the same community today, where the grandsons carry on.) Had there been a default, which there rarely was, Grandfather would have made the loan good.

As a youngster, I was often aware of the reactions of friends and neighbors to Grandfather's presence. Never was I conscious of anything but the most profound respect for this man who kept his promise. This integrity was also expressed in our attitude toward work, particularly if the obligation were to others. On threshing or butchering day, for example, it was a matter of pride to be there before the whistle blew or the first pig killed. It was a matter of integrity not to soldier on the job. When I was thirteen I wanted to escape the prosaic tasks common to the farm and go threshing instead. Before my first day's experience, my father asked me if I thought I could do a man's work. He warned me that he never wanted anyone to ask why Elmer Eby sent a boy to do a man's work.

My grandfather taught me one of the most significant lessons of my life. We had been threshing oats all day, and the work was smutty and dusty. Late in the day, as the sun was going down, we were cleaning up beneath the feeder—one of the dirtiest and dustiest jobs imaginable. Disgusted, I stepped back and let others equally tired do my job. Seeing me leaning on my shovel, Grandfather, then an old man, took it from me and did my job. Later he explained, kindly yet firmly, "Kermit, a man always helps clean up." Since then, whenever the going gets tough in politics and government, or even in my family or church, I hear my grandfather say, "A man always helps clean up."

Grandfather's attitude toward work was almost exactly that of Rabbi Joseph, the builder. Both were working ministers, responsible for their flocks, and both believed that a promise imposed profound obligations on the one who made it. The Torah tells of a rabbi whose opinion was once sought on a certain matter. The questioner found him standing on some scaffolding and said to him, "I want to ask you something." The rabbi's answer was, "I cannot come down because I was hired by the day."

Among the Brethren this sense of responsibility was more than personal. It also had its social manifestations. For example, there was no more irresponsible neighbor than he who let his Canada thistles go to seed, for the wind blows the seeds hither and yon, and endless hours of backbreaking labor are needed to keep them under control. Sometimes, if a neighbor were careless, Grandfather and Dad went to him and offered to cut the thistles before they bloomed. Grandfather, as a neighbor once said, was known "as favorably for the cleanness of his fence rows as for the eloquence of his sermons." And Grandfather would have been as proud of the former compliment as of the latter.

The same social responsibility was expressed in our care of the streams which ran through our farms and of the roads in front of our farms. The good farmer kept his stream cleaned out so that it would not clog up and flood his neighbor's fields, and he filled the mudholes in the road in front of his home. Those were the days when we worked out our road tax. Today we simply pay it.

This philosophy of responsibility was best expressed in my ancestors' attitude toward the land and its products. These men believed it to be their responsibility to God and their fellows to leave their farms more productive than they found them. They regarded themselves as stewards of the good earth. What they received from their fathers was to be passed on to their sons.

My father's farm, bequeathed to him by my grandfather, is more productive today than it was forty years ago. No government agent had to teach Dad that surface water washed away topsoil, or that hillsides and gullies should be sodded over. He learned this from his ancestors, who brought the first crop rotation and clover crops to America.

To this day Father has a reverence for the land. He likes to feel it in his hand; to see it glisten, black and rich, behind his plow; to share its lifegiving impetus as he walks between the rows of corn. Dad always insisted that it was sinful to sell straw, and seldom were the economic pressures on him strong enough to tempt him to sell hay. You bedded your animals down with the one and fed the other to livestock; and twice a year you covered your fields with rich manure. Father believed that if you robbed the soil, sooner or later it would rob you. To this day I feel that my father's deepest scorn was reserved for those who wasted the soil. And even now, as I see eroded countrysides, I shudder at the blindness of men who cut their trees, flood their streams, wash away topsoil and so hasten the making of dust storms and deserts.

It is an easy transition from respect for the land to respect for its products. Little need be said of the excellent quality of agricultural products grown by Pennsylvania Dutch. What impresses me is the integrity of character which kept my ancestors from putting the biggest apples or the smoothest potatoes on the top of the basket. Doing so would destroy the discovery of the goodness underneath. Their products, like their lives, were better the deeper they were penetrated. For example, my father never left any runts among the fat hogs he sold. He always culled them out himself because runts were a reflection on his ability as a feeder. As a consequence he often received a price better than the prevailing market price. His potatoes were so carefully culled that I often thought of the poor and hungry who might live off our seconds.

Historically, the Mennonites and Brethren were among the sects known as "withdrawing." They believed that the world is evil and that they could attain their ideals only by living in the presence of God and therefore separate from the world. There was never any question in their minds about primary loyalties. And they believed that the witness of the life was more convincing than the argument of the word; hence they were little given to disputation. It is exactly here, it seems to me, that their strength rests, for ours is an age inclined to judge by outward appearances.

Our Brethren historians tell us that early Brethren settlers moved into a frontier settlement, built their homes, created their communities and depended on their daily witness to spread their way of life. This seems a better way to influence life than all the argued homilies of the evangelist.

There is no substitute for integrity, and the more complicated the society, the greater the need for men whose yea is yea and whose nay is nay. There is a subtlety in both the Brethren and Mennonite positions which transcends the obvious integrity relating to family life, to the farm, to the job. Both Mennonites and

Brethren refuse to swear an oath. To be asked to do so is an af-
front to their personal and religious convictions. It was taken for
granted in the world of my boyhood that a liar could be depended
on to swear to his lie. As Mother sometimes caustically remarked,
"I wouldn't trust X if he swore on a stack of Bibles." As I get older,
in these years of the oath, I am more and more convinced of the
rightness of those who swear "neither by Heaven; for it is God's
throne: nor by earth; for it is his footstool: neither by Jerusalem;
for it is the city of the great King. Neither shalt thou swear by the
head, because thou canst not make one hair white or black. But let
your communication be yea, yea; Nay, nay: for whatsoever is
more than these cometh of evil."

Integrity of life transcends any and all oaths. Such a position
is difficult for others to understand. Time and again, as I attempted
to explain my reluctance to swear an oath, I was told, "What difference does it make? Go ahead and take it." And I must reply:
"That is exactly the point. If it makes no difference, why do it?
And wouldn't taking it without meaning it debase its coinage? For
me there can only be one answer."

I wish there were more who understood this attitude. If there
were, I am sure that less confidence would be placed in either professional informers or professional oath-takers.

It has always been my position, when called on to swear my
loyalty to state or nation, that my life should be witness enough—
and if it is not, no oath could make it so. Here I am in the Brethren tradition. Nor would I hesitate to answer any question about
my life and activities, so long as my answers do not implicate another person. The ethic does not permit either tale-bearing or
passing judgment.

Underlying this Brethren belief is the assumption that those
well-grounded in the faith need not fear other doctrine. Should a
Brethren or Mennonite associate with a Communist, it is just as
likely that the Communist would be converted to the simple life
as that the Mennonite or Brethren would become Communist.

After all is said, this respect for integrity is a respect for the
values by which a man lives. What has always impressed me is not

that men are proselytized by false doctrine, but that an emptiness of soul gives such easy virtue. No, Grandfather Schwalm would not swear to tell the truth; he was too wise to take the oath, for he knew that the temptation to lie comes before the necessity to affirm the truth, and he preferred to begin where the temptation arose, in his own mind and heart.

4. Education for Sectarians

The most paradoxical experience of my life occurred when I was dismissed from the examination room of Senator Jenner. I had said there: "I am now, and have been since 1927, a Brethren minister whose interest in peace took him into economics and other related fields." My membership in a church which was once hounded from Europe because its brethren refused to kowtow to Caesar was for Jenner a badge of respectability! Doubtless Senator Jenner knew how the modern descendants of those European refugees are inclined to vote.

If we Brethren knew our heritage, believed it and testified to it, our church itself would be brought to trial. And I believe that the primary purpose of a church-related college is to emphasize that heritage so emphatically that it becomes a part of the intellectual and spiritual life of each student.

My experience on Brethren campuses in the last few years and my contact with Brethren students on a graduate level convince me that this is not the case. The Brethren students do not know the history or the reasons behind the beliefs they profess. Hence, they are easily assimilated into the ordinary materialistic life. Such assimilation may be justified in an ecumenical age on the ground that they are the leavening of the secular lump. But where will the leavening occur when there is no longer a sectarian fount to give it birth?

If I were a Brethren educator, I should be avowedly sectarian. Otherwise, why be a Brethren educator at all? I am convinced that our heritage contains particular values which are of monumental importance to our whole society: our emphasis on a rediscovery of Jesus' teachings; our emphasis on the transcendent evil of war, and especially of a world war which offers us not only personal but

22

generic death; our understanding of the futility of the oath; our emphasis on the integrity of life and contract; and our conviction that it is more important to win the man than the case. These are the values expressed in the magnificent drama of the washing of the feet, which we repeat among ourselves, that drama in which the suffering servant is the central and triumphant figure.

I plead for education which gives Brethren youth and all youth a pride in their special heritage and a sense of historical continuity. That continuity is a precious gift, and it begins with an understanding of the kind of world our rebellious forefathers lived in. It is a satisfying and healthy thing to remember that our Brethren ancestors also faced the horrors of totalitarianism and war and that they came up with alternatives to both.

As a Brethren educator, I would make it my purpose to develop tough-minded students—men and women who are conscious that they are destined to be in conflict with the world. I might even conduct a course on the great heresies. The course might include the study of Christ, Erasmus, Luther, John Huss—yes, even Karl Marx. I would teach Brethrenism as an heretical doctrine, and I would make a persistent attempt to find out why we produce so few heretics. For years I have been trying to discover why English Pietists (Quakers) were social agitators, while German Pietists (Brethren) were so often conformists. Is German authoritarianism more a part of our heritage than many of us like to admit? My final emphasis in such a course, therefore, would be on the fact that for every heretic who emerged triumphant and for every revolution which succeeded, history shows a dozen failures.

Our own comparatively successful experience with democracy has made many Americans forget a few basic facts about politics. Because of our own national birth in revolution against England, we are taught to revere the martyr. We are also taught that if a cause is righteous it is bound to win.

John Stuart Mill pointed out in *On Liberty* that the evidence of history refutes this idealistic view:

> History teems with instances of truth put down by persecution. If not suppressed forever, it may be thrown back for

centuries. To speak only of religious opinions: the Reformation
broke out at least twenty times before Luther, and was put down.
Arnold of Brescia was put down. Fra Dolcino was put down.
Savonarola was put down. The Albigeois were put down. The
Vaudois were put down. . . . Even after the era of Luther,
wherever persecution was persisted in, it was successful. In Spain,
Italy, Flanders, the Austrian Empire, Protestantism was rooted
out. . . .

My course on history and heresies would be geared to produce men and women willing to act on their convictions, even when
there is no assurance of success. A Brethren school, conscious of
its heritage would be, by definition, in constant conflict with H. L.
Mencken's "bitch-goddess, Success."

It is at this point that American education has perpetuated a
fraud. We have come to think of the educator as an apologist for
society, a foreman in an ideological factory retooling the bright,
questioning students so that they will serve the status quo. But a
good teacher is not a claims adjuster for any system. Rather, he is
a questioner, a man of both thought and passion, an agitator. And
on the highest level he may become a disturbing prophet. Jesus
of Nazareth spoke quite clearly on the subject: "They that are
whole do not need a physician." He also stated that there is no
virtue in putting new wine into old wineskins.

The institutionalization of Jesus as the Christ is an old story:
the psychological entombing of the leader and the nullification of
what the leader taught. When Rome could not destroy Christianity, it embraced, modified and finally corrupted it. The technique
has not been forgotten. Today, in Moscow, the bodies of Lenin
and Stalin are kept on perpetual display, with embalming fluid as a
final ironic tribute to the beliefs that impelled them. In America
we have embalmed both our religion and our teaching, along with
the Declaration of Independence, the original of which is on display in Washington, and an exact copy of which dozens of people
in Madison, Wisconsin, refused to sign not long ago on the
grounds that it "sounds communist."

The spirit of Rotary has taken over both our religion and our education. From the small, comfortable churches in the hinterlands to the high, comfortable churches of the city, the businessman is given great comfort in his endless search for security. Christ has become a sweet and amiable soothsayer, a legend which fearful old women and timid young men may safely trust.

Sectarian education brings no assurance of success, as society defines the word. There is no promise of upward mobility, salary increases or status satisfaction. Actually, the accumulation of such rewards is often only the measure of our compromises.

It is the responsibility of teachers in sectarian schools to prepare our students for worldly failure and to make them conscious that the Cross is the inevitable destiny of all who would follow Jesus. Our goal is not peace of mind; our goal is the ability to live with our tensions.

In these Brethren schools I would look for professors whose business is to profess. These professors would be open-minded. But open-mindedness is not absolute: every man who is mature compromises within principle, but there comes a time when compromise, even within principle, is impossible. These professors would also test their values in the laboratory of life. Realizing that such men are hard to find and hard to keep, I would try to protect them. There could be no compromise with academic freedom.

Few indeed are the men with courage to hire men more brilliant than themselves, and after hiring them, to protect them. The temptation of the strong is to make themselves the sun and those they hire, their planets. History is replete with such examples. When such strong men depart, the institution reflects its emasculation. But strength should produce strength; courage should be contagious.

Athletes who place their physical prowess ahead of their intellectual attainments would find no home in my school. Winning teams and spectator sports are just one step removed from the bread and circuses of ancient Rome. I would not be party to a conspiracy for recruiting players or paying coaches a higher salary than their scholarly colleagues. The present athletic programs of many universities are, of course, frauds: they pretend to be amateur, and they almost never are. American societal values break down when our youth sees the contradiction between the extolling of the truth and the awarding of success to those who practice the lie.

Finally, it is my opinion that sectarian schools should place men ahead of monuments. All over America it is easier to get money for buildings than endowments for scholarships. How many big stone churches are being built to glorify man at the expense of men? Let us spend only half the amount for buildings and, with the other half, give secretaries to ministers and educational directors, who might then spend more time in study and meditation.

Brethren schools should be prophetic, unapologetically visionary, havens for the dissenters in tension with the world—sectarian and proudly so. Otherwise, why Brethren schools?

5. Like unto Our Heroes

As Carlyle has pointed out, men need heroes. If they do not have good heroes, they will follow bad ones. Gandhi and Hitler are, in that sense, equals in the scale of history, for they both fill the need of man to follow, to emulate with the passion of conviction.

The true aim of any society is to survive and, following survival, to secure cultural self-perpetuation. To that end, a society must produce heroes who will serve its aims. If the society is in need of men to manufacture goods and more goods, the values will be work values and the heroes will be work heroes. Thus our home-grown American myth-men are superproductive. John Henry could drive more steel, Paul Bunyan could cut down more forests, than any man alive.

The myth-man is an outsized representation of the hero, and the hero, an outsized representation of the actual human being. Beowulf was a human who became a hero and ended as a myth. The dragons he slew were symbols of Anglo-Saxon man's collective fears: sloth, deprivation, the threat of starvation, force utterly untrammeled by law. Beowulf's dragon is none other than the ghoul which always sits glowering and half-hidden beneath the table of civilization, ready to overturn it and to appear again in the light of day whenever too many people get careless. Men eat at the table of civilization, always aware that the ghoul watches them from beneath, bearing in his hands all the ugliness of barbarism. In another and more terrible sense, the ghoul sits deep and hidden in the heart of man. Quite often, as at Dachau and Büchenwald, he emerges in all his primeval slime.

Thus each generation invents its own heroes to slay the same dragon which appears and reappears in new forms. Each generation must train its children to be socially useful. The simplest, most effective training is given by example.

The hero is a useful tool in this training because he embodies the main threads of pattern and custom. He is a living personification of the virtues which a society desires its children to emulate. George Washington is said to have always told the truth. A careful and unbiased reading of the life of George Washington reveals certain deviations from the path of pure virtue. But what matters to the teacher is that the children should see the large shadow of truth cast long against the walls.

But the shadow is more difficult for an American child to see than for those born into more homogeneous cultures. Dr. A. Cohen writes in *Everyman's Talmud:*

> The principal responsibility that rested upon parents was to train their children for their life as members of the Community of Israel. The ideal aimed at was to forge them into secure links in the chain of continuity so that the religious heritage which had been bequeathed by the preceding generation might be transmitted unimpaired to the generations which would follow. The indispensable requisite for such a consummation was the instilling into them of a knowledge of Torah.

The Torah was the unilateral way, the life, the tree of knowledge. It was the book of heroes and of heroic acts around which an entire culture might knit itself. It was the refuge against persecution and pain; more, it was a handbook of the variety of ways in which a man might learn to live in the world and conduct his affairs.

For the American public school child, there is nothing similar to the Torah. Hardly an American believes in the Bible. Both Protestant and Catholic believers have to send out missionaries to their neighbors as they once did to the heathen in other lands.

There is no real chain of continuity in America. The famed melting pot is no melting pot at all because there is no primary culture into which the Slav, the Pole, the Jew, the Negro—and especially the Negro—can melt. Further, any minority man who succeeds in becoming integrated loses his uniqueness. What he gains is a membership in the local Rotary club and a chance to voice the same patriotic, businesslike phrases as those of a thousand other colorless voices around him.

The factors which tie all Americans together are not cultural, but ideological: nationalism and democracy. Of all the political systems men have created, democracy is the most subtle and the most complicated. Democracy demands the ability to compromise and to see many issues at once; it means a system in which power is diffused among many interrelated pressure groups.

Thus, the ideal democratic hero is very cautious about drawing his sword against dragons. The dragon may have some good in him after all, and further, the dragon might represent a significant pressure group. On the other hand, the ideal democratic hero must have a deep face of conviction, a principle in mind. Otherwise he would be no hero at all, but an opportunist. As F. Scott Fitzgerald succinctly phrased it, the ideal democratic hero must "hold two opposed ideas in his mind at once." The ideal democratic hero might very well be a combination of Huck Finn, that precise blend of suspicion of humanity and love of humanity; Will Rogers, who used the mother-wit of his suspicion to create the folk-wit of love; Franklin Delano Roosevelt, who betrayed his aristocratic ancestry by becoming a politician; and Henry Adams, who bemoaned the fact that his patrician upbringing gave him too much insight to be useful in politics.

No such hero, of course, has appeared upon the scene. The official hero is a man with a Rotarian heart and the face of George Washington—a hero who must absorb all cultures and colors, so that in the end he has no color and no culture at all. His emotional tone reflects a middle class which not only wants to include all races, religions and cultures, but also to make over all races, religions and cultures in its own image.

This tone of emotional neutrality may account for the change in the older generation's attitude toward the younger generation. There is much less thunder about what the younger generation is coming to and much more wonder about what it is not coming to. It is middle-aged men who call the younger group the Silent Generation; and even with the various purges of educators, college professors still note with some surprise that their colleagues are more radical, more ready to take a chance, more ready to explore possibilities than the great majority of their students.

The chief characteristic of the Silent Generation seems to be that it holds as a positive virtue the ability to blow neither hot nor cold. Thus, when the sorority girl dates the fraternity wheel, both avoid involvement until they are ready to marry. After marriage they continue their relationship with as little involvement as possible. Once such people might have been called cold; they are now termed stable. The Silent Generation has taken too seriously the parental admonitions to settle down, be cautious and don't get into trouble—a series of negatives which, if they were to become the dominant emotional tone of society, would succeed in making that society as static as a pharaoh's tomb.

Indifference is, of course, not the only attitude. There are too many Americans for the Rotarian-with-the-George-Washington-face to swallow up in homogeneous vapidity. There are far more Americans than the public school teacher can forge into secure links in the chain of continuity. For there is no chain of continuity, nor is there a single book such as the Talmud to give to our society a distinct tone or a precise, positive depth. The public school teacher has only an American flag (which cannot be accepted by the children of Jehovah's Witnesses), a picture of George Washington (which may be disavowed by those Negro children who are aware that Washington owned slaves and treated them poorly) and perhaps drawings of Sir Galahad and the Gleaner. In addition, of course, he has the textbook. Not to offend any religious sect, the school administration binds the teacher to a textbook that will help him to teach cultural do's and don't's without distasteful philosophic curiosity or moral commitment. Instead of religion, the textbook teaches a distilled and anemic brand of kindness. In short, textbooks teach morals in a moral vacuum.

A patchwork of half-digested ideas, outright half-truths and profound inconsistencies underlies American thought in lieu of cultural continuity. The child must be taught at one and the same time that it is good to be friendly and good to be successful, good to better himself and good to be kind, good to be cooperative and good to be competitive. Meanwhile, the child's real heroes are elsewhere, among the cowboys and sharpshooters who know good from evil and slay their dragons without compunction. The person who exemplifies moral ambivalence is the one who stands before his classes each day and communicates to his students whatever he can glean from his own cultural heritage—and too often what he gleans is no deeper than a preference for people who bathe every day, or the conviction that the most important thing in life is to get along with people, to be friendly, to continue in the way of the innocuous.

Meanwhile, the American child learns daily that his survival in the actual world depends upon knowing not only good from evil, but the first-rate from the third-rate. If he goes into adulthood with no better philosophic base than his schools teach him, he may live out his life utterly insensitive to the thousand cultural pressures around him, and certainly insensitive to the dark and tangled threads which are at the core of human motivation.

I once had a bright and sensitive student from Gary, Indiana, a Negro who decided to study the effects of public school education upon the Negro community in Gary. He equipped himself with a wire recorder and went back to his home town, settling himself in bars and hotels, in meeting places and on street corners. The record of the sometimes aimless, sometimes forthright, conversations he brought back showed one thing clearly: none of the people to whom he talked was prepared for life in America as America really is. The majority of the people he talked to were factory workers. Their education, which seemed to have been directly oriented in middle-class values, had inculcated all of them with the vague idea that anyone of worth becomes a doctor, a lawyer, a dentist, a writer, a schoolteacher, a small businessman, if not a corporate executive. They had also been taught the traditional public school Abraham Lincoln story, that any man who wants to can become President. Few of them had wanted to become President; all of them had dreamed of becoming independent, professionally or in business.

In the maw of economic necessity the false dreams soon faded. And no real dreams took their place. Suspicion of humanity conquered love of humanity, and they became men without heroes; the official hero who was given them to emulate came not from their own strivings but from ideals of people living in an altogether different situation. So far as we know, there sprang no heroes from the heart of the medieval serf either; for the official medieval hero was a warrior-knight who, to slay his dragons, had to be perched on the upper one-tenth of the social ladder. The majority of men who labor are aware that they are without swords, and even if a man has the surplus energy, the dragons are too big to be killed—as big as a monopoly or a cartel.

Where, then, is our democratic hero? We have our official myth-man: the Rotarian-with-the-George-Washington-face, clean and well bathed, odorless and sentimental. But he seems to inspire no one. He is never seen slaying a dragon, unless it is the vague dragon of un-Americanism, a dragon which is all things to all men.

A much more representative American myth-man is not the good Rotarian, but the fallen Rotarian, Willie Loman from Arthur Miller's *Death of a Salesman*. Willie Loman, like the Gary factory workers who found their dreams chimerical, also got tripped up in a double-minded value system which attempted to make him act morally without believing in morality. Willie Loman sincerely wanted to be good; he believed that he should get ahead and at the same time be well-liked. He would have genuinely liked to slay dragons, had he been able to recognize one when he saw one.

In the end, of course, the values by which he professed to live betrayed him, offering him no sustenance, not even an old-age pension. But perhaps his real tragedy lies in the fact that his life had been one long sin of omission. It was like the life of that other fallen hero Peer Gynt, who, slowly peeling down the onion which symbolizes him, discovers that the onion has no heart.

6. The Cruelest Decision

When he was thirteen years old, Allan Haywood was sent down to work with his father in the coal mines of Yorkshire. Miners in those days went into the pits before daylight, and came out after dark. At thirteen, Allan saw neither the sunrise nor the sunset. There was no day, only darkness lit by lamps in the mines.

One day Allan's father took him by the hand, saying, "Today we do not go to work at the mines, but to hear Kier Hardie." Until the day he died, Allan remembered hearing the voice of Kier Hardie in the coal pits.

America, the land to which Haywood migrated, was the scene of layoffs, speed-ups and incipient industrial strife. The close community of the mines was always made more tense by the possibility of sudden and explosive death. To many of these miners, as to Haywood, unionism became a kind of religion. When Haywood married, he built a house in Taylorville, Illinois. In the latter part of his life, he returned there only once or twice a year, for the union filled more and more of his time. When he went from town to town, the regional directors met him and set up meetings for him. After the meetings, they drank with him. The meeting hall became his home, and the miners' children, his family.

At sixty-four, Allan died as he would have wished—making a speech to union men. They took him home to Taylorville, a stranger. The men who carried his coffin were members of CIO; the men who wept were miners who knew him in the meeting halls. Hardly anyone in Taylorville really knew anything about the man named Allan Haywood.

For Allan's life was like the story told about St. Francis of Assisi. The saint went to the snowy mountains, molded himself

33

a wife and children from the snow, and wept because he had no family. But then, looking over Italy he said, "These are my wife —these my children."

And yet, among all those who are dedicated and single-minded, Allan Haywood was a comparatively simple human. I remember the train rides we took together, and I remember Allan drinking too many beers on occasion. Indeed, if there is veritas in vino, Haywood had, beyond all the speechmaking and all the politics, a warm heart and a soul more than once bewildered. For on those comparatively relaxed train trips, Allan remembered the voice of Kier Hardie, and perhaps his remembrance evoked a terrible feeling that Kier Hardie's words had been buried deep beneath too many speeches, too many train trips and too many power struggles. But others I have known were not so warm. They succeeded so well in becoming im-personalities that they were able to live by a code which states coldly that kindness does not constitute morality.

If kindness did not constitute morality to these men, responsibility did. For at least one whom I remember, the larger responsibility ruled out all his primary relationships. His name was Sol. Socialism and Zionism had become his family, his community, his children. He taught mathematics in a small college when I knew him, and in the evenings he gave lectures on the cooperative farm system (*kibbutzim*) in Israel. He was a small man, and the malnutrition he had suffered in one of the Nazi pogroms in the East had stunted him physically. His immediate family had been wiped out in gas chambers. He did not expect to marry, and he showed no self-pity about this. I have never known a man so utterly alone, and so quietly alive with the flame of the one love, the one dedication, the one loyalty.

Someone remarked to me the other day that the final war would break out between the Communists and the ex-Communists. It was intended as a witticism, yet the comment contained a grain of truth. Real war goes on between *kinds* of people, in a different and more meaningful sense than between nations. Perhaps the final war will be fought either by disillusioned fanatics against those who are still fanatics, or simply by the believers against the unbelievers. There has always been a struggle between those who are dedicated to a cause and those whose chief goal in life is to be let alone. Of the latter, some are apathetic or afraid or both. But others are civilized men in the traditional sense. Traditionally, civilized men have always considered themselves too well-balanced emotionally to adhere to any one cause, victory or defeat.

I once had a student friend who epitomized the spirit of the civilized. Joe was a slow, careful man, fond of good wine, good food, pretty women and artistic flower arrangements. He was studying Far Eastern culture. One day I asked him about his reasons for preferring this particular subject. "Well," he said, with his usual affable smile, "I am studying the Far East because—one must be interested in something, you know."

I believe that Joe honestly felt no need for larger ideals. In this he differed from another of my young friends, Sumner, who was perhaps equally fond of good wines, good food, pretty women and art. I talked with him on the eve of his departure for an army draft call. Like a number of intelligent young men, he was not eager to enter the army. He had no enthusiasm for the war in Korea, which he believed to be a false and meaningless combat between two great imperialistic nations. But Sumner would have liked to have had enthusiasm. "Take Socrates, Pericles and the rest," he told me. "Then there was something for which these men could be genuinely patriotic, a standard to which the just could repair, a fight for a real home, a real idea. Now? Today? It is not so, and I wish it were."

I do not believe, as Sumner appeared to, that the decline of any given culture can be traced to the triumph of the civilized and apathetic over the dedicated and singleminded. The truly dedicated are always in a minority. There are always many more who, like Sumner, would like to find something worthy of their whole and intense desire, but cannot although most men never view their lack of one strong love and one strong desire as a problem.

I arrived at a deep understanding of the peculiar dilemma which Sumner faced when I received a letter from the wife of one of my former students who was working a seventy-hour week as a union education man. Music, art, books, the quiet evening at home had disappeared from his life. His wife asked me to plead with her husband to stop this kind of life and go into management or college teaching. There he might also work effectively for the cause of the worker, she argued, and he would again have time for leisure.

I replied to her pleas with great hesitation: "I understand. But I would not suggest your solution. Because for a man to be a man at all, he must follow the gleam as he sees it."

Many have followed the course which the young wife suggested. In recent years young men have deserted not for more money, power or prestige, but because they felt that the unions were no longer a standard to which the just could repair. Some of them, considered too radical for the unions, entered management. As one of them explained to me, "Now I have a nine-to-five job, no Sunday conferences, no meetings lasting until three in the morning, and furthermore, what petitions I sign and what meetings I attend after office hours are my own business. Management doesn't give a damn because it can afford not to care about such shifting and fickle political winds."

But others have grown to crave strong emotion, just as some men prefer well-spiced meat; they could not leave the movement so long as it fed their craving. Some time ago I became nostalgic with an old friend, a UAW man who had stuck with the union through all things. For men like him, it is hardest to stick out the fat and prosperous days. Like myself, he remembered the auto workers marching, thousands strong, down the streets of Detroit. We recalled the great days of the 1930s, when the strikers put newspapers under their caps to protect their heads from policemen's clubs. And once a man has seen such things milder meat no longer whets his appetite.

For such men, homes and families become mild meat. Labor, politics and high-pressure management are filled with the wreckage of men who went out, built their lives, broadened their own experience and were unable or unwilling to take their wives along.

The result was that children of labor union leaders were brought up in middle-class environments, filled with a vague form of middle-class philosophy, and sent out into the world with no awareness of or interest in their fathers' profession. Someone once told me that he knew of no second-generation Communists in America because Communists were so busy saving the world that they had no time for their children.

It was precisely that extraordinary devotion of the old-line Communists which earned them the dislike and fear of those who fought them. Communists were thought to be tireless, utterly decisive and completely disciplined. They could outsit you in meeting, outtalk you in caucus, outwork you at the mimeograph machine and outbelieve you every day of the week.

The real problem of the Communist in America is not the question of conspiracy, but the fact that there are few men in any society who are willing to be responsible for it. Apart from the professional politicians, only eggheads, gangsters, Fascists and Communists participate seriously in American politics. The intellectuals participate from conscience, the gangsters from desperate necessity and the dedicated Communists and Fascists from a wholehearted desire for an absolute standard to which the just can repair. The sheer, cold fact about the dedicated is that they are sure of their premises. They know how they want society to be run, and they are willing to take the consequences of running it. The tragedy of communism is that many who dedicated themselves to it discovered that it was, at best, only a standard around which the superman or sub-man might rally.

The deepest emotion controlling the lives of the absolute saints who seek complete inner power, and the absolutist leaders, who seek complete power over other men, is a disgust with the purely human. For such saints and leaders, life is full of mistakes and retreats, ambush and idiosyncrasy, inconsistency and absurdity, alarms and excursions. The struggle of a few men to become saints and supermen is a straight fight, a fight for abstract love or disembodied hate, fought with pure power and without inconsistency.

The cruelest decision, then, comes when a man must choose either the power and the glory or the simpler, less exciting meat; the common pleasures, the pursuit of family harmony and the planting of rose bushes. Those who are unable to realize themselves either in the struggle for power and glory or in the struggle for humanhood are the real failures. Those who choose one may yearn for the other or may disregard the other as a snare and delusion.

Lenin objected to the symphony because great music made all life over, mellowing a man and making him want to pat the bourgeoisie on the head. Lenin understood that there, waiting in the woods, were Pan and Peter Pan, Dionysus and the Fisher King, Thoreau contemplating nature and a man contemplating his navel.

In order to secure for the children of the world their sunrises and sunsets, perhaps it is best to have no children of one's own. Perhaps it is true that only the rootless, the excommunicated, the Spinozas and the Christs are strong enough to give men roots, communication, communion.

7. Why Labor Leaders Are Lonesome

The labor leaders I have met are lonely men. They are lonely as they address the great rallies of their followers, lonely as they manipulate them in caucus and convention—yes, lonely in their plush offices, surrounded by sycophants and secretaries. But they are most lonely when compelled to spend some rare moments by themselves. For it is then that they come face to face with their past and recall the idealism of their youth, the shared sufferings, and the hopes for a new and better world.

Many times, as I listened to the top dozen of America's labor leaders speak, I have closed my eyes and tried to imagine what they were like as boys and young men, years ago, before the symbol erased the man.

What was Philip Murray like when he slapped the checker at the mine's mouth, when he tramped from home to home organizing the miners, when he read and listened to the words of Gene Debs or when he chose to share the little that was his with others who had even less? Or John Lewis, face to face with the problems of his family and his friends, striving to better himself so he might help his community of miners—what was he like? Or Allan Haywood as he listened enraptured to the eloquence of Kier Hardie —what kind of a man was he?

I knew Walter Reuther in the early days of CIO in Michigan. He was a worker among workers, a dedicated dreamer, approachable, winsome, willing to listen. Many times as he pounded home his point to men at auto and CIO conventions, I pictured that other Reuther, the off-stage one, the one who in 1947 came to the Atlantic City convention to address the young ministers we had brought there, describing to them the opportunity for service their calling offered. As he spoke, he evinced little of the tension which characterized his presentation as he spoke to the CIO delegates some fifteen minutes later on the challenge of communism.

I do not expect the Lewises, Murrays, Greens and Reuthers to turn back into the men they once were. Labor leaders do not return to their past. Usually, only death liberates them from the present. And as they live, they accept the role of indispensability forced on them by lesser men who depend on them for security and status. Was not John L. Lewis indispensable to the CIO until peculiar circumstances relieved him of his indispensability in 1940? Did not Philip Murray inherit that mantle of indispensability? And wasn't Walter Reuther their heir? Who else could hold the CIO together? Who else could ward off the destructive impact of lesser men, jealous for his powers and prerogatives?

In all of life there is nothing more arresting than to see a man captured by and made the servant of his own public image. Such a man is set apart. People glance in his direction when he walks the street. His services are provided with an extra flourish. His name is referred to on radio and in the press. Inferiors flatter him. God-like, he learns to dispense favors and withhold rewards—lift up and cast down.

Yes, it is exciting to be a public figure, to stand a few inches above the crowd.

Perhaps the top labor leaders would hold on to their jobs less anxiously if the world from which they came and to which they would, if compelled, return were more attractive. Men who have met and jousted with the great of the earth do not voluntarily return to coal mines and punch presses.

Labor leaders are lonely—lonely in the presence of their pasts, lonely as the symbol triumphs over the man. To climb the heights in union organization, a man must have few doubts. The conflict of soul which those doubts produce would make him impotent. Decisions cannot be unmade, nor actions undone—a strike called, a rival crushed, a staff man fired, a wife and family sacrificed. Seldom, if ever, can one risk being more interested in any single person than in the organization. I know. One of my own secretaries told me, in the last year of my stay in the CIO, "You used to be interested in my problems, how I was getting along with my boy friends, but now when I try to talk to you, you look up at the ceiling."

I am not going to say much about the family breakups among those in union and political circles. In one sense they are inevitable. Men who climb to the top in great labor organizations begin as dedicated men and end as kept men.

It is very difficult to be politic for ten or twelve hours a day, to live with crisis and catastrophe, and not to resent being plunged into new crises on arriving home. A real letdown takes place from the time the leader shuts his office door until he arrives home. A sympathetic wife, he reasons, should understand what burdens he carries; so should the children. Never, never should he be asked what he wants for dinner, or be disturbed by a son's demand for the car or a daughter's request for a new party dress. Instead, wife and children should learn to wait on him as his secretary does or, if he is a big shot, as his staff and their secretaries do. But members of a family never do. They are human. Ultimately the father ceases to be a part of his family's daily interests and decisions; the relationships settle down into a stalemate of frustration or end up in divorce.

There is real tragedy here. The leader who has made the union his life has little else to talk about. Often, pressed by loneliness, he seeks fulfillment with others equally dedicated and equally captive. A secretary who shares his office life begins to share his private life. If the director of the organization attends a meeting in a strange city, the regional directors, almost as rootless as he, can rent a room in his favorite hotel, stock it with liquor and regale him with his prowess as a leader. But neither mistress, whiskey nor stooges ever really overcome the deep loneliness, for it is a loneliness of spirit.

The labor leader is lonely because once at the top, he is no longer a man among men. He is a demigod among mortals who aspire to be demigods, the apex of a pyramid toward which each in his own way aspires. Furthermore, any shift at the top means a dislocation in all the ranks below. So the rivals are in the ambiguous position of being compelled to support that which they consciously hate. It is inevitable that the leader lives in a world of tension where lesser men bid for his favors and secretly damn him as they accept them.

None of us, I am convinced, loves a man who has the power to humiliate us. By calling on someone else to make the historic speech at a convention or by forgetting to include us on a trip to the races, he puts us in our place. We no longer respect ourselves when he does not respect us. We cheapen him and ourselves, contributing not only to the leader's loneliness, but to his lack of information and his consequent errors of judgment as well.

There is no more intellectually stultifying experience than being surrounded by flatterers who fear to speak their minds. Royal courts once welcomed fools who dared speak honestly, for these fools protected the ruler against his own close advisors. We produce fools, but they speak according to formula and protect nothing but their own soft seats.

This seems to me the profoundest argument for rotation of leadership. It is too much to expect men to speak as equals when their security and advancement are at stake. Mutual distrust prevails. As people ask to see the labor leader, he wonders what they want—what gossip concerning a rival is to be passed on, what favors will be sought for friends or relatives, what special pleading will be made for some favored person or project. Knowing the delicate balances among his followers, the leader plays the ambitions of one against the other, and as they checkmate each other, he continues to rule.

Theoretically, staff men are expected to base their counsel on fact and foresight. They are supposed to be above the battle. But they rarely are. The smart staff man, interested in his own survival, learns what the policy is and what the boss wants. He, too, has ambitions for a larger staff, for increased opportunities to see the boss and thus advance his own private interests. Often these boot-licking staffmen are more despised than the political fawners—probably because they have so little power. When they do have ideals which transcend their self-interest, few other people believe it.

The Sunday before I left the CIO, I did a broadcast on a subject which was very dear to me—increased educational opportunity for America's children. One of my political superiors heard the broadcast and stopped into my office to congratulate me. "You really believe what you said!" he commented with surprise.

The moral is obvious. The prevailing pattern is so taken for granted that the exceptions are not received seriously and usually make but little impact. Unfortunately, the pressure on top leadership is so great that there is seldom time to meet simply to talk or to share creative dreams. In union circles, there is always a crisis impending or a catastrophe to be avoided. The structure of the great unions is such that almost all questions must be resolved by the chief. Philip Murray moved from questions of state to the bickering of staff men and the quarrels of secretaries in one short hour. For him there was no escape. Perhaps the day will come when books, music and art will be part of the conversations of men in power in the labor movement, but that time is far away.

The secretaries of union big shots invite a study all their own. Most of them are persons of great power, dedicated to the perpetuation of that power. There is no better way to do this than to contribute to the isolation of the boss by making him difficult to contact. After all, he cannot be very important if anyone can see him, and if he is not important, neither is his secretary. Even in the minor spot I held, I was once criticized by a secretarial protector for my ease of approach. Furthermore, it did not help her status among her peers to have a boss who went out into the hall to welcome callers. If a boss is naturally distrustful, a secretary who discreetly contributes to his suspicions will make his isolation complete and his loneliness overwhelming.

On special occasions the results of these patterns emerge most clearly. At Christmas parties, men call each other by their first names, join in group singing and try to achieve for a brief hour what they do not have throughout the year. Sometimes there is more consciousness of status and awareness of difference in the simulated camaraderie of special occasions than in the easy formality of the everyday world. At least, this has been my experience.

When I sojourned among the AFL men, where the term "brother" was used in addressing fellow officers, the form was present but the spirit long since dead.

The union movement is no longer a fellowship of dreamers sharing one faith and aspiring to a common destiny. Today, big unionism is big business, and its power structure resembles that of the corporation. Abilities are demanded of its executives and experts similar to those demanded of executives and experts in big business. Orders in both worlds usually pass from the top down. Senior executives support those subordinates who are loyal rather than those who are competent. In a sense, there is a class structure in the union world, determined by power, prestige and income, much as there is in the corporation world. The world of mine and factory, of dingy union halls and indigenous protest has long since passed away. Efficiency has conquered enthusiasm, statistics have won out over men. Brotherhood grows out of community, never out of hierarchy. Naturally there is loneliness.

There has been too much speechmaking at union conventions. The orator, the man who speaks to the crowd and sways it with his eloquence, is a man apart. His audience is merely an instrument on which he plays. He is a lonely man who seldom has the opportunity to hear his opinions challenged. It would be better for him and for the movement if the organization were structured so that the leader sat at a round table and exchanged ideas freely and equally with his fellow workers.

A sense of humor might also be helpful. Occasionally, in the midst of some peroration, I find myself laughing at my own seriousness. The ability to laugh at ourselves insures a fellowship of equals. If we doubt our own infallibility, we must include others in the circle of our need. Once the circle is established, communion is not possible without love. And love demands our acceptance as persons, apart from all titles and prestige, apart from all the externals of office. We are accepted for what we are—yes, in spite of what we are.

Labor leaders are lonely. As long as big government and big organizations exist, men will be set apart and lonely. Recognizing this, I cannot but feel that those set apart must be governed by a true humility which is rooted in the soil of everyday living. Then they will be willing to return to the people who produced them.

8. On Workers' Education

Not too long ago I made one of my few trips back to a union education school. I spoke about one of the primary concerns of the workers: their relationships to their fellow men and to their union. The workers gave my speech an ovation. They cried, "Go ahead! More!" I think it was not my particular brand of bread which excited these people but their own unfulfilled hunger.

The continuity which is theirs, I said, is a precious heritage. The security which is theirs was won by the struggle of their predecessors: "the blood of the martyrs is the seed of the union." I described for them their early history: Pengelly Hall, the vigilantes, the police brutalities, the sacrifices. I told them that their heritage goes back through the AFL, the Knights of Labor and the cordwainers; and back beyond that to Spartacus, the Christian martyrs and the ancient lowly who protested making bricks without straw. They cannot step out of this continuum even if they want to.

I believe that labor history and labor heroes are an important part of workers' education—and particularly those heroes who are dedicated to more important goals than perpetuating the bureaucracy and living on an expense account. To those who argue that history is removed from the lives of men, I reply that it is not necessary to seek into the past; it is only necessary to begin with specific men at a specific point in time. Ours can be described as a world of impersonal forces, one in which the individual is increasingly overwhelmed by the multitude of problems and the complexity of organizations. The increasing numbers who stay away from labor meetings are those who no longer believe they can affect their own destiny. This is why I would teach labor history. As we sense man's struggle and feel the drama of life, we tend to identify ourselves with our fellowmen, to become sensitized to them, and to experience what Whitman describes as the joy of comradeship.

The continuity of history can be taught through the belief that each man, working with his brothers, can shape his own life and the lives of his brothers. It is not by chance that men have always died more gladly for the vision of the kingdom than for the gadgets with which they implement their vision. Not all the convenient patent gadgets will give men their basic satisfactions. Those who built the labor movement saw visions and dreamed dreams. They saw every man under his own fig tree, at peace with his fellowmen.

Workers' education, too, is full of its own emphasis on techniques—the gadgetry of teaching. Quite often, with such technical competence, there may be complete absence of any meaningful content, above all, of any attempt to know and understand the surrounding environment. Walter Lippmann has phrased it well: "We have established a system of education in which we insist that, while everyone must be educated, yet there is nothing particular that an educated man should know."

The men of our factories often take the Horatio Alger dream of America with them into the world of the assembly line, the union hall, the ruthless industrial system. To many of them, therefore, the real world never becomes actual. The obsession of an ill-fitting and outmoded dream and the guilt in not being able to live up to it can prevent a man from seeing reality.

In such a situation, the union hall is, for the worker, one of his most tangible means of continuity. But because he has no idea of what to expect from such a fluid community, he often treats it as something automatic and irrelevant to his life. Only a vital union program of induction might make this community meaningful to him. Union membership today is too limited: the signing of a card, toleration of the checkoff, the taking of benefits do not provide meaning. The objective of a workers' program under such circumstances should be to furnish prospective members with a sense of history before they join. The checkoff itself, which is so automatic, destroys the values of dues books and stamps; like all indirect taxation, it moves away from involvement and toward isolation.

The educated man, Robert Hutchins once said, is he who sees the total consequence of his actions. It becomes increasingly difficult for men chained to one small assembly-line process to see the total consequences of that process. Men take refuge in the corner bar, so that the bar in America becomes a kind of mock community of frustrated and lonely men. Real communities are based on the idea that an individual, working singly and with other men, can affect situations and events. He responds and the situation responds.

Often the union fails to create real community. It fails by emphasizing mechanical matter of checkoff. It fails when, through organizations such as the International Federation of Trade Unions, it concentrates so much time in working for world community that it neglects the grass-roots community out of which the movement itself originally grew.

The union fails when it cannot successfully replace the sentimental myth of Horatio Alger with a real and vital dream. When a man goes into the factory world and is forced to put aside the myths of his adolescence, he will remain in a vacuum until he discovers a more vital commitment. And unless there is a commitment for him to discover, he will remain in a vacuum all his life. Men do not risk their lives and livelihood in a strike, or in any battle into which they enter voluntarily, for anything less than a vision. How vividly I recall the fierce utopianism of those who built the CIO. Not only did they have their own dreams, they were sometimes jealous of rival visions. They were singing, vital, morally committed men.

9. Organization, Bureaucracy, Loyalty

In the six years with the CIO, I was always careful to register my title as Director of Research and Education, rather than the reverse, Education and Research. To those who know the labor movement, the reason is obvious: research has bread-and-butter value. Education does not have such tangible and demonstrable uses. Early in my career, I decided to do as good a job as possible in bread-and-butter areas, so that I might plead for tolerance, if not support, on the educational part of the job.

Even before I came to the CIO, my heart lay in the work of education. With the Teachers Union, I advocated the professional development of teachers and detailed their community responsibility. I knew, however, that there would be opposition from the countless teachers who did not want to be disturbed in their routines and who pictured the Teachers Union as a streamlined AFL building service operation. My misgivings were dramatically affirmed on one occasion when a delegation from the union came into my office and reminded me that I was employed to represent their economic and job interests before the Board of Education and before the public, not to reform the school system nor to concern myself with teaching methods.

He who would understand union administration must understand the pragmatism which governs the behavior of its leaders, a bread-and-butter philosophy which springs from the rank and file. This pragmatism is the despair of many Europeans and a few Americans who believe that the trade-union movement cannot exist without a philosophy of reform. I confess that, although I understand the nickel-an-hour approach and have gone along with it, I believe that man expresses himself in his function, in the job which he performs.

Walter Reuther may be known as a dreamer and a dangerous radical, but to the members of the UAW he is the man who put them out front in wages, pensions and job security. He can make speeches about the rice fields of Asia and the social responsibility of business; his followers tolerate these excursions into the irrelevant only because he has delivered the goods to them when it counts.

Phil Murray, the tolerant father who permitted his staff to concern themselves with the whole world of reform, summarily pushed aside all side shows when contract negotiations came around. Phil believed that as steel goes, so goes the nation—in wages, security and production. While he went along with Sidney Hillman's Political Action Committee and many innovations of the modern trade-union leader, he believed that a union's strength is economic, that its total responsibility is to get the best deal it can for its members.

Lewis's career is an even more dramatic illustration, for while his followers repudiated him politically, they never repudiated his economic leadership: in this area, Lewis delivered.

The labor world is a legalistic world, a world of contract interpretation, a world of fine print. It is much like the world of a corporation lawyer. It is, in fact, the lawyer who is present in the last steps of negotiation. He deals out the figures which the research men and economists make available. Consequently, little love is lost between the two types of specialists. The economists sow what the lawyers reap: kudos.

There are more tangible rewards than kudos for trade-union lawyers. Almost without exception, they are on a salary scale of their own, and what they receive bears no relation to the salary of other department heads. The argument runs as follows: "Look at the sacrifices we are making by working for a union! Think what we could make if we were representing a corporation." And the argument is quite readily accepted as valid. Economists, publicity men and legislative representatives do not seem to be able to sell their talents for nearly so high a price. It follows that their

•

rewards and sacrifices are considered, in direct proportion, not as great.

One of the deepest impressions I took away from the CIO experience was the memory of Phil Murray walking down the hall at 718 Jackson Place to the back end of the building where the law department was located so that he might confer with Lee Pressman and Arthur Goldberg. When he wanted to confer with department heads, he called them into his office, but not the lawyers. For lawyers are hired to keep you legal; and sometimes, because they do, they know where the corpses are buried. The only time I recall Murray in a cynical mood about lawyers was on a day when he suggested that the Taft-Hartley Act should be christened Lawyers Full Employment Act, written by lawyers, interpreted by lawyers and contested by lawyers.

I tell my students that if they want first place at the round table next to the chief, they should study law. The senior member of a law firm can ultimately go to Congress, while the junior member can look after the firm's interests.

If the lawyer is the most powerful staff member among union administrators, the most powerful official is usually the director of organization. The director is doubly powerful if he combines an elective with an administrative position, as did Allan Haywood of the CIO.

Organization is, after all, the life blood of the union. There is nothing for a union to do, functionally speaking, except to expand its membership. Since the inception of the CIO, its organizational growth (with the possible exception of the period before the Korean War and the 1958 recession) has ridden an escalator. Membership has expanded along with our economy, and actual organization of the union in new areas has not been difficult, except in the South.

Since 1940, the great labor organizations have been growing by natural accretion more than through the impetus of history or their own activity. Consequently, the organizational staffs have had more than a little time to consolidate their political positions

•

and to strengthen their own structures. Each man found his place in the political structure and helped to strengthen the union. Whenever possible, these men also attempted to undermine rival unions. This accounts for the cannibalism in the trade union movement. From time to time, efforts have been made to end these jurisdictional disputes, but they have never met with great success.

Among other things, the organizational staff is the haven for the brokendown political hacks of the trade union movement. The staff is usually large enough so that the incompetence of a few can be covered by the competence of many. It is only just that a man's present flaws be overlooked in favor of his heroic organizational triumphs in the past. But in the smaller departments, where the contact between chief and staff is direct, it is not easy to cover up a failure.

Whenever there is pressure for funds from rival departments, the director of organization has an unanswerable argument: "How many dues-paying members do you bring in?" Neither the research director, the legislative representative nor even the lawyer has a ready reply. Nor can one prove with consistent effectiveness that education will eventually strengthen membership.

Unions, like corporations, prefer to operate in the black: the more members, the more dues, and the better the financial statement. The International Ladies' Garment Workers Union and the Amalgamated Clothing Workers are so wealthy that they are sometimes in a position to help maintain the solvency of the business with which they negotiate. Each year, as I read the reports of the AFL-CIO, I note that its assets are on the increase. Ironic indeed is the contrast between deficit financing in government and union economic practices.

The union is like the corporation in other ways. Efficiency in administration is admired in both organizations; line and staff in both are almost military in their hierarchical delineation of responsibility.

The first lesson a union staff man learns is where power rests; if he doesn't learn that simple fact, he doesn't stay a staff man very long. To question the Lewises, the Meanys or the Reuthers is to question the gods. And how often have I seen the look of shock on the faces of the lesser satellites when one among them had the temerity to contradict or even question his superior.

My own bitterest internecine battle followed a situation like this. As executive secretary, I challenged the president of the union and was ultimately dismissed under charge of insubordination. During that struggle—and even today—members of that union insist that I was guilty of heresy.

A sociological study of these factors might reveal that unions are conditioned by the society which produces them. Table pounders produce table pounders. The Amalgamated Clothing Workers cannot be understood unless one understands Hart, Schaffner and Marx. The steelworkers take on much of the sociological coloring of United States Steel, and the automobile workers are not unaffected by the composition of General Motors.

As a consequence, the modern American trade union is an institutionalized service organization which may be judged by the splendor of its building, the competence of its staff and the success with which it represents its members. Its voice is as close as a long-distance phone call can bring it, and its spokesmen are never more than a few hours away by plane. Its technicians are as competent as their counterparts on the other side of the collective-bargaining table, and their speakers are often more eloquent.

Those who now seek careers in unions are more often asked to display their technical competence than their missionary fervor. Sectarians may be fine, but you can't use them in the auditing department. In spite of twelve years of union experience, I would not be at home in the pension division of a large union—the technical demands are far beyond me. The young man who wants a career in the union today looks forward to it as he might to a career in business. He prepares himself in accounting and law, gets himself a contact and finds himself a niche. The pay is good, and if our hero can make himself indispensable enough and colorless enough, the security is first rate.

The bright young man, if he wants to get along, should also

have one or two ideas. The most recent triple play has been from wages to pensions to annual wages. The number of people who understand the complications of the annual wage can be counted on the fingers of one hand.

There are more variations in the salary schedules of union officers than in the schedules of their business counterparts. In the CIO, whenever we argued that there should be some salary equity, Jim Carey argued that salary schedules were undemocratic and that men should be rewarded by the contributions they made to the CIO. Of course, Carey was judge of those contributions, and he occasionally confused loyalty to himself with loyalty to the union.

One of the fictions which developed in the CIO as a result of line and staff organization and the emphasis on loyalty was that top officials preferred to deal with department heads, not with anyone of lesser rank. This emphasized the cleavage between those who had arrived and those who had not. Thus any memos to top officials were signed by department heads, who were responsible for their contents. And so the fiction was kept alive.

The rewards followed the fiction. A department head could always be fired at the wishes of his superiors, but he was king in his own domain. Within the limits of numbers, he could hire and fire as he wished, bound only by his sense of human values and ethics. A department head could appear at the inner council of officers where he was treated almost as an equal. He could travel without question, and his requests for advancement were honored. Not so with the lesser lights: they entered the Holy of Holies only on rare occasions, and they took their turns for free trips to the conventions. Of course, this was not an absolute—there were occasions when indispensable secretaries went along with their chiefs to Europe and other far-off places.

An understanding of union administration means an understanding of the emphasis on interpersonal loyalty, and especially of loyalty to the man ahead of you in the power hierarchy. This is the loyalty of the battlefield, where the security of each depends upon the unity of command. When one faces company pressures, police pressures and societal pressures, it is important to know that the men at one's side are unquestionably loyal.

Psychologists have fun analyzing human identification. Some of us identify upward and some downward. Perhaps those who work in the union bureaucracy should be psychoanalyzed before accepting a position; if they don't identify upwards, they shouldn't apply. It is not easy to learn to be a ghost writer, and loyalty is the indispensable virtue in such a task. When one does not respect the man one step up in the hierarchy, irreconcilable conflicts develop.

Yet a man, to be a man at all, must be loyal to values which transcend a personal devotion to his chief. There is an incompatibility between loyalty to the hierarchy and loyalty to the democratic ideal. My theory of administration has always been that departments and organizations are healthy only in proportion to the disappearance of the status differentials. That is why, in the departments which I administered, everyone came to meetings and had a voice in determining policy. Each understood that he was important to the whole, and the *esprit de corps* was high. Yet this sort of organization was interpreted as a weakness: the Director of Research and Education was dependent upon assistants, associates and lowly secretaries. In an organization which used the word for propaganda rather than as a plumb line for life, an attempt to take the democratic ideal seriously produced tensions which ultimately led to liquidation.

10. Democracy through Decision

In administrative relations, as in all human relations, obsequiousness is debasing. So is condescension. Only a relationship in which men accept their integrity as men is worthy of emulation. A good society would contain no elite and no men of low estate, no masters and no slaves. As Roman history so vividly demonstrates, masters who make other men their slaves must in turn accept enslavement by those above them.

Because the Romans regarded slavery as the basic institution of society, nothing prompted them to say no to a man who claimed to have owners' rights over them, or to that man's heirs, whose property they became by inheritance. A Roman citizen might commit suicide upon receiving an order; a slave could not commit suicide because that would be robbing the master. Historians tell us that Caligula kept a row of senators dressed in tunics standing behind him at his meals. The tunic was the characteristic mark of slavery. At banquets he had the habit of absenting himself for a quarter of an hour, taking a noblewoman to bed with him, and then bringing her back to join the other guests, among whom was her husband. These people, who beat not only their slaves but their colonial peoples, had no other course but to accept their own degradation.

As the Romans looked upon slavery as divine, so we tend to regard working for the boss as divine. In the psychological sense, we, too, are often slaves. Note the number of out-and-out despots active on the American scene, in management and labor alike. To these people, their fellow men are merely numbers in the production or dues-paying process. We all know this sort of overtly hostile and deeply authoritarian type. Indeed, we look upon a certain kind of willfulness as colorful; we do have a certain kind of respect

for John L. Lewis, for example. We reshaped our ancestors' authoritarianism into the institution of rugged individualism.

But what does the existence of such types really signify?

In *John L. Lewis—An Unauthorized Biography,* Saul Alin-
sky describes the break between Lewis and Phil Murray after
thirty years of collaboration, thirty years during which Lewis com-
manded and Murray obeyed. Breaking with Lewis was one of the
most traumatic experiences of Murray's life. For months Murray
was physically and psychically ill; only the constant affirmation that
he, too, was a man gave him any sort of reassurance. Long after
the break, "Lewis remained the ruling force in Murray's life,
either because of Murray's previous allegiance, or by his later
all-consuming hatred."

Men who consent to slavery for a long period of time find it
difficult to call their souls their own. There is a story, which may
be apocryphal, to the effect that one labor leader sent the wife of
one of his staff men a dozen roses on their first wedding anniver-
sary in atonement for his absence at the wedding. Flowers for the
subservient, but professional death for the independent, has always been the law of despots. The corporations not only demand
the loyalty of their executives' wives, they employ psychologists
to measure the wives' loyalty before the executives are promoted
or hired.

It was this confusion of loyalty with subservience which
forced me to leave the CIO. The final incident concerned a
woman employed by the CIO and assigned to my Department of
Research and Education as an editor. One day during the legislative session of 1947, it was necessary for us to work overtime on a
testimony for Phillip Murray. Late in the afternoon, this editor
chanced to drop into Mr. Murray's office, where the secretaries
were loafing while their bosses were out. She made a violent and
profane remark to the effect that if everyone did her share of work,
others wouldn't be forced to stay overtime. Murray's secretary
reported the incident to Murray himself, and Murray ordered one
of his subordinates, James Carey, to fire the editor. Carey did so
with vehemence and dispatch: "Just get the hell out and stay out."

No charges and no reasons were offered; there was no union representation of the accused worker.

When the editor came to me, as her superior, I took up the case with Carey. I asked him about union standards applying to union employees, and was likewise threatened with peremptory dismissal. I then went to see Phil Murray. I pleaded union ideals. Murray replied that the CIO—yes, even the steel workers—had confidence in me, and why get so bothered about an insignificant person when there was so much work to be done building a world in which workers were secure. I replied that I felt it useless to work for the whole at the expense of an individual member. After several hours I was assured that something would be done. Nothing ever was, even though I pushed the matter every time Murray came to Washington. Staff men simply do not win victories over elected officials.

Three times in my life I have come into violent conflict with organizations to which I belonged—each time because the organization had violated the principles it claimed to represent. I have defended individual men against institutions because it is the man who dies, the man who suffers, the man who creates.

Each man has a desire to identify, to become part of other human beings. This desire is an actual need, often suppressed, overlooked, cheapened or commercialized, but a need which is, in varying degree and intent, felt by all of us. This need may, in rare individuals, reach the proportion of an obsession; to identify becomes the need to *be* the other person, and may border on the saintly or the demonic. St. Vincent de Paul was once a traveler on a galley. His fellow passengers, wealthy and respectable, ignored the slaves below the deck. But St. Vincent went below, saw one of the slaves dying from overwork, and so identified with him that he took the oars and rowed for him.

This need to identify totally with other human beings is not confined only to the greatest saints or the greatest sinners. It exists in the tortured artists and writers like Arthur Koestler, whose experience in the Communist party was one long, frustrated desire to absolve himself of both personal and impersonal guilt. André

Gide, whose guilt, like Koestler's, was based on an upper-middle-class upbringing, gave up membership in the party, not because communism treated him badly, but because it treated him too well. As a foreign celebrity visiting the Soviet Union, Gide was given the same preferential treatment that he was trying to escape in the capitalist societies of Europe.

As hardheaded men, we so often underestimate man's need to identify with other men and his need for idealism. Yet we know too much about the hidden springs of motivation—or, at least, we have been able to guess too much—to be satisfied with the simple, selfish Hobbesian explanations of man's behavior. We know about such things as the will to self-defeat, for example; we know that it takes a very well-integrated person (or a very sick one) to be able to work for himself alone. We know a little about the close correlations between vanity and self-abasement, between the desire to identify and loneliness, between the desire to give and the fear of human closeness.

The chief fault of most bureaucracies is that they do not recognize these paradoxical facts. Because of its very nature, a bureaucracy must view man as an animal to be manipulated. But the manipulation is seldom very subtle. The effects of intense manipulation of large numbers of men may be perfectly horrible, as under the Nazi regime, or amazingly stultifying and depressing, as under the Soviets, or simply confusing and demoralizing, as so often in the United States. Here we have not so far resorted to state instigated terror as a means of manipulation; we have used silence, censorship and distortion or suppression of facts. The McCarthys and Jenners never seemed as great a threat to our liberties as the well-meaning bureaucrat who is afraid to let people know the truth, who withholds facts for our own protection. It is too dangerous, these men feel, to reveal the actual dangers of hydrogen bomb warfare.

Suppression of information, slogan-making and a kind of double-think constitute the main temptations of the bureaucratic existence; and such bureaucracy creates a feeling of apathy or confusion in most of us. We feel more and more that we cannot affect our national destiny, certainly not by using the government's administrative structure. Even during the so-called isolationist era, Americans generally showed more excitement about national and international issues than they do today.

I think it has always been difficult, but not impossible, to give meaning to the Judaeo-Christian ethic within the world of administrative power, a world which is becoming more and more remote from those affected by the power. In our time, attempts to apply this ethic have not been particularly successful. Cooperatives and unions depend upon power relationships and status differentials. The attempt at a communitarian outlook, as represented by suburbia, has resulted only in new and more colorless conformity.

Small communities bound together in a common ideal of the good society was a Brethren idea. I do not think that such communities can exist in today's world, but the only alternative is the increasing depersonalization of man. That depersonalization seems to negate both real individualism and deep identification with groups. Intensity of in-group feelings and factionalism seems to us clannish, sectarian or unrealistic.

The Brethren envisaged a community of communities, each in turn built of ever smaller communities, the basic cell being the cooperative and the family. The Brethren would have agreed with Martin Buber: "But if individualism understands only a part of man, collectivism understands man only as a part. . . . Individualism sees man only in relation to himself, but collectivism does not see *man* at all, it sees only 'society.' " These ideas have played a large part in radical Catholic social thinking, and are beginning to influence Protestant thought as well.

Communitarian I may be, yet I continue to live in Chicago instead of abandoning the world to move to a Brüderhof in Paraguay or a Hutterite community in the Dakotas. Why? First, I don't have the courage to make such a move. Second, I believe that there are no islands, and that two or three ideal communities scattered here and there over the world will not solve the problem.

I would rather face the old dilemma of trying to bring what exists more into line with what should exist.

Since most decisions have to be made in the world that does exist, it is better that the sensitive and idealistic get into the positions where these decisions will be made.

My own policy as an administrator was to attempt to build around (1) joint decisions, (2) open channels of communication and (3) shared benefits.

To begin with the first: the idea is advanced more and more that joint decision is impractical in the world of large organization and delegated powers. With this I disagree, and my experience in World War II with labor-management production committees strengthened my conviction. Determined to defeat Hitlerian fascism, we introduced a bit of democracy in the industrial process, only to discover that it worked: there was a direct correlation between the degree of cooperation and productivity increases. Ironically, once Hitler was defeated, there was less need for joint discussion, and cooperation was abandoned as too utopian. However, postwar studies confirm the wartime experience.

Both in the Chicago Teachers Union (as executive secretary from 1937 to 1942) and in the CIO, I found that if a supervisor were accessible, if he had time to listen to grievances, that very act relieved tensions within the organization. The good steward was the fellow who left his channels of communication open two ways: between his men and himself, and between the foremen and himself. The history of Ford's transition from industrial war to industrial peace was the history of the demise of Harry Bennett and his strong arm spies, and the introduction of a functioning stewardship system.

Because I believe in shared benefits, I have always argued for open-book negotiations. Without all the facts, it is impossible to develop responsible unions, for one cannot negotiate in a vacuum. Open negotiations naturally lead to some form of profit sharing. Oddly enough, the greatest difficulty I ever had in making the case for shared benefits was before a group of Mennonite businessmen. These men were willing to give Christmas bonuses, but absolutely unwilling to negotiate them with their workers, even the workers who were fellow churchmen. In this case, the paternalistic drive overcame the communitarian.

In the CIO, I was head of a department which was responsible to the president alone. Philip Murray could fire me at will, but, just as he had absolute power in his kingdom, I had absolute power in mine. Whenever possible, I hired staff men who shared my viewpoint and my outlook on what I wanted to do, but since much of the staff was inherited, it was necessary to blend the convinced and the unconvinced. This was done by holding open staff meetings, which included everyone from the newest secretary on up. We had no secrets; our ambition was to create a situation in which it was assumed that no one person had a monopoly on facts or intelligence. To insure that all information was available, both office and executive correspondence was available to everyone.

If individuals act upon their knowledge, they must be assured that their actions will be supported. There can be no buck-passing. But even more significant, everyone responsible for a memo, testimony or speech must receive credit for his work. As department head, I did not play the game of omniscience. I read my assistants' drafts and collaborated with them, but our superiors knew that these were joint efforts.

In the CIO, I found it necessary to develop clear and open understandings about salaries, raises and incidental rewards, such as trips to conventions. The CIO national office operated on other principles: department heads and policy men were advanced or their salaries determined by personal whim, or as a reward for their bargaining abilities, or incidental to the introduction of a new favorite with a higher salary into the official family. James Carey said: "I know best each staff man's contribution to CIO, so I determine what he should be paid." The system was one of playing the serfs off against each other. Once a favorite was brought in at a salary two thousand dollars above all other department heads. The rest of us were offered raises in placation. When I remonstrated and refused a raise unless my staff was raised commensurately, I was accused of being disloyal to the elite status. When told that I would be raised willy-nilly, I insisted that I would divide the raise among my staff. This finally compelled some adjustments.

The big event each year was the national convention. All but a skeleton staff of secretaries went. By making it clear that seniority, not favoritism, would qualify secretaries for the convention, I removed another major grievance area.

My basic desire, then, as an administrator, was to establish an atmosphere of trust and fairness. I am sure now that people work much better in such an atmosphere; furthermore, it seems to me difficult to work with men whose word you cannot trust. In administration as elsewhere, the idealist may often prove the most practical of men, that is, *if* he has the control and knowledge to be able to work effectively in the world as it is.

11. Labor and Political Action

"The unions of America belong to their members." Fine words—but saying so does not make it so. In fact, if we can judge by the utterances of union leaders, the unions belong to the bosses. They call the strikes. They deliver the votes. They make the decisions. The great multitudes of workers are not the generating source of decision and action. They are merely the social base on which the leaders' influence rests. The union is to be played upon like a pipe organ, manipulated as a juggler manipulates his pins. In times of emergency, the workers are expected to be radical, but never so radical that they are uncontrollable, never so powerful that they cannot be shifted in a twinkling of an eye from one line of support to another.

The reasons for the situation are many. Here are a few of the most pertinent. The modern trade union, like the modern corporation, is monolithic, a huge, human shaft of power directed from the top. Its conventions are attended by professionals—"pork choppers"—who must support the men above them in the power hierarchy because their present and future security depends on the maintenance of the status quo in power relationships. Decisions which affect the rank and file worker are being removed from his own hands: the decisions are technically so complicated that only the expert, or the leaders advised by the expert, are competent to make them. And finally, too much union education is based on steward training that prepares the worker to handle only the minor matters on a local basis. Performance, not the ability to question and criticize policy, is the criterion of a successful union education program.

What can be done to reverse this trend? To begin, we must reach those individuals who will become union members long before they are ready to join. Their union education must begin when they are young.

We must ask the home and the public school to prepare the future member of Local 264 more adequately for his job as a union man. In the first place, parents and educators might begin by assuming that little Johnny is likely to work for a living. More likely than not, he will work with his hands. It is the job of home and school to develop in the young a proper sense of the dignity of labor. Instead of implying that education will help Johnny live off the sweat of other men's brows, we should encourage in him a proper sense of the honor and fitness of doing his part in the world's work. Few textbooks stress the social significance of postmen, carpenters and factory mechanics. One would think that first-class citizenship in America belongs only to owners and executives, foremen and superintendents.

We might concentrate more on training our sons and daughters for citizenship, not in some far-off post of honor and power, but in the local clubs and unions. In school, at home and in union locals, there is no reason why young workers-to-be should not learn public speaking, parliamentary procedure and political organization. Today, I am told, the high schools are plagued by drop-outs. I would suggest that the curricula be revised to treat civics and social problems in the first two years. Now, such courses are given during the last two years and reach only those who need the training less than the drop-outs.

The curriculum and all its allied activities should be related much more closely to the actualities of life. The problems in arithmetic might be built around payroll deductions, wage regulations, charge accounts and housing costs. There is no reason why civics students should not discuss union bosses, checkoffs, free-riders and strike benefits. Our more alert school leaders are moving in this direction already, though generally these subjects are considered too controversial to be discussed. Parents—and that includes union members—neglect the job of encouraging an alive and meaningful education.

We have not begun to tap the resources of union leadership.

We bring local businessmen, professors, and doctors to our classrooms as examples of responsible citizenship. Why not bring the local union leaders? We must urgently reorient ourselves in this respect. We hurt our nation when we encourage emulation of prestige which is not based on the dignity of all labor.

Free spirits cannot be developed under the guidance of the slave-minded. How can we expect the pupil growing up in an authoritarian atmosphere to be other than authoritarian? Public schools and homes should redouble their efforts to develop youngsters who are unafraid of ideas, who are loyal to their values and who are not easily made victims of boss rule. The future union members of America must be capable of questioning.

For the task of education, free men welcome allies. The kind of education needed to make unions responsible organs of democracy can also come from other organizations: Sunday schools, clubs, young people's meetings, churches. But there is a danger in accepting the aid of groups whose prime loyalties are not to democratic process and the theory of union, but to bases outside the compromise structure of liberal democracy.

I deny the churches the right to interfere in internal union affairs. To work from an external base of loyalty is to frustrate democratic behavior. The proper function of churches in relations to unions, I believe, lies in another field entirely.

Workers need meeting places. This is especially true of the unorganized workers. In most cases, the organized workers have already established their own halls and clubs. But if they had meeting places more socially desirable than washrooms and bars, they might use such places for genuine democratic discussion and problem solving. Why could not church basements be used as workers' clubrooms, with television and organized discussion groups?

Why should not men dedicated to religious faiths work in plants and share the hopes and aspirations, the disappointments and frustrations of their fellow workers? Here the opportunity for Christian service is most evident. The spiritual influence should be direct influence of contact and example. One person ministering directly to the workers on the assembly line would be worth a thousand pulpit-bound pastors.

The churches should exercise power with labor, not over it. In the words of Jesus, a pastor can become the yeast which, losing its identity in the lump of dough, leavens it and brings forth bread. This is no mean assignment for a man who describes himself as religious. He must go into a world in which the culture, language and activity are unlike those of ordinary church service. He may know great loneliness at first. But the alternative is to preach in the mission house on the mountain top, where the birds are the only creatures that listen.

Except for spiritual guidance of individual members and the creation of a climate of friendship and brotherhood, the churches have no place in union affairs. They can provide training in democratic process and encourage their members to be good union men, but they have no right—and should have no privilege—to interfere in union practices or objectives.

The impact of environment on the union member is just as telling within the union as outside it. Let me not be misunderstood: I believe that the union member wants his union. He remembers what life was like before unions attained power. But except in times of emergency, the average union member prefers to go his own way, drink his beer, work his garden, bet on the horses and gossip with his neighbors. In this attitude he is much like the average churchman, who thinks churches are fine for the community but are not part of his personal life. Both unions and churches are treated like insurance policies—one a protection for the here; the other, for the hereafter.

If there is one attitude more prevalent than any other in unions it is apathy. And apathy is directly related to the size of the union and the complexity of the major decisions it must make. Power which affects the individual member is too far removed for him to get excited about. God is in His heaven and the leader is in national headquarters!

In view of the prevailing size and complexity of the organizations, I do not believe that oratory about democracy will materi-

ally affect the situation. If anything, the trend is in the opposite
direction. The unions are getting larger, the bureaucracy more en-
trenched. But we can dream, can't we? And in our dreaming, we
can project better choices.

Obviously the average worker cannot become technically
competent enough to understand all the intricate fine points in contracts and the Taft-Hartley Act. Nor does he need to do so. But
he can understand the basic policy decisions on which more detailed decisions must rest. The worker is no fool. He can and
must be trusted to determine the basic policy within which his officers and their technicians should operate. This is the basis of
democratic government.

The preparation a worker needs for acting on policy grows
out of his most immediate concerns. Myles Horton, formerly of the
United Packinghouse Workers of America (CIO), introduced
something new in the field of workers' education. His program
called for an education shaped by the union members' own immediate problems and led by the workers themselves. No outside
experts are to be called in. Instead, it is assumed that men living
with men in a union have common concerns. From discussion of
these, the program moves to wages, to contracts, to stewardship,
and finally to the relations between officials and local membership,
and between locals and the national and international offices. The
workers' knowledge and skill increase with this discussion and
study.

This program works. Already the regional heads of unions
are protesting this new kind of worker education which upsets the
status quo, and are asking a return to a safer brand. Here is proof
positive that the workers are becoming skilled in handling their
own affairs.

Years ago I was invited to teach in the automobile workers'
summer school in Michigan. At that time, the great tension between two factions of the union was reaching its height. Walter
Reuther's rising star was challenging the Thomas-Addes incum-
bents. I had no sooner stepped into the camp when a man to my
right asked, "Are you for Reuther?" He was interrupted by an-

other on my left asking, "Are you for Addes?" Naturally, I replied, "I'm for Murray." I knew enough not to be caught in a factional fight.

The first session of school was opened by a Reutherite. His address was tinged with factional considerations. The school administrator, anxious to escape an open fight, asked me if I could do anything to get the class started on the right foot.

I began by asking the workers to forget Reuther and Addes for the moment: "Let's call one X and the other Y. It is reported that X is an ex-Socialist, a social planner. Y is a Communist, or at least a favorite of the Communists. Now, what does X stand for in the union and the nation? And what does Y stand for?" We went down the line, listing the differences, real and imagined. We moved from personalities to ideas. The evening class lasted three hours. After class, the workers held a meeting and voted to give me full time to go on with this teaching method. For two days and nights I rallied all I knew, beginning with X and Y and going back to Debs and Marx, Jefferson and Hamilton, Machiavelli and St. Francis—yes, even to Aristotle's discussion of politics and Plato's views of the State. And everyone went with me. When it was time for me to depart, the class gave me an ovation.

Why?

Simply because their situation demanded clarification and decision, and the education I offered was related to their immediate realities. Every man present believed that he was going to be called on to make important decisions back in his local. He, as well as Reuther and Addes, was someone.

Let us look at a contrasting situation. It may tell us something of what unions should become.

The 1952 labor delegation to the Democratic convention was one of the most ineffective political units ever assembled, not because of any lack of personal worth in the individuals, but simply because of the kind of operations they were expected to perform. In the first place, their designation as labor delegates placed them in an ambiguous position. Actually theirs was a larger constituency, a community one. In the second place, when they came to the convention, their instructions were: "There are three good candidates—Stevenson, Kefauver and Harriman. Agitate for any of them; knife nobody; and if there are further orders, you will be notified." Translated, this meant that Phil Murray would get the tip from President Harry Truman and pass it on to Jack Kroll, after which all the little jigsaw pieces would fall into place.

For almost three days there was no message. Rumors ran high. Indecision and foolishness marked the efforts of our delegation. The labor leaders called for the defeat of Vice-President Barkley because of his age. Shades of William Green, Matthew Woll, John L. Lewis, Phil Murray and the other union youngsters!

Finally, it was obvious that Governor Adlai Stevenson was the man. A caucus was called and addressed as follows: "The bosses have decided on Stevenson. He will be nominated on the third ballot. Represent your constituents on the first ballot. If the break comes on the second, climb on the bandwagon. It must appear that he is our candidate as well as the bosses'." The delegates followed orders.

Is there an alternative to this machine drill way of handling the matter? Yes—responsible group action on the spot, democratic majority decision and support of that decision by the leaders. In the school I conducted, the men acted as men. In the 1952 convention, they were puppets, emasculated by a system contingent upon one man and his contact with the President.

Ideas are not enough, of course. They must be realized in cell, caucus and political opposition. Men in unions must be permitted to give political form to their diverging ideas. More rank and file discussion is needed, especially when official policy is reversed by the leaders.

We must look forward to the day when ideas in unions project themselves into parties, and when parties create the tension which motivates progress. Otherwise there can be no alternatives but dictatorship, or rebellion against it by some almost equally powerful political dictatorship, or the splitting, collapse and destruction of the union.

Before any really democratic progress can be made in the

unions, the umbilical cord which connects American labor to Washington must be cut. This does not mean that political action should cease. On the contrary, it is a public duty of unions to engage in political action. The unions have a vital role to play in furthering the whole society's democratic growth. They are a very large segment of that society. But the unions must be independent of political favors and responsible on their own account.

Labor grew with the New Deal and the Fair Deal. A liaison evolved between the Great White Father in the White House and the little labor fathers. Except during strikes and elections, the chiefs found it easier to go to the White House than to the rank and file.

Such a relationship was convenient but dangerous. If the President and his party become increasingly dependent on a particular segment of the population, the inclination to favor that segment increases. There have been times when big business treated Washington as an adjunct of Wall Street. Labor leaders, equally power-minded, are capable of believing that the government—and not least the chief executive—owes them something. When Washington yields to either side, government no longer belongs to all the people.

Today, labor's relation to the party structure on which our political system rests is ambivalent. The major unresolved issue today is the relation of the labor movement to the Democratic party. The question is whether the dog will wag its labor tail or the labor tail wag the dog. The resistance of the regulars to newcomers and their brash, assertive ways so far has kept the dog in command. But the tension promises to increase as labor's power increases. Sooner or later, the role labor is to play in political life must be examined seriously.

I contend that here, too, the answer lies in local labor organization. On the community level, where voter and party worker meet, where the daily compromises are made, union interests and national interests can be adjusted. If they are not adjusted on the local level, the conflict can lead only to division between labor and its natural allies and to the emergence of a labor party. Such a development might be healthy. It might be good for labor to be forced to assume national responsibility. It might be an excellent thing for labor to carry just one city so that responsibility would go with its power.

As it now stands, labor has no final responsibility, but it still has a powerful influence on the party system. Unions are now powerful enough to accept mature obligations and to function not as destroyers but as builders. They can do this only when they match their practices within the union to the democratic formulae of the American system. If unions do not form a political party, they have the obligation to work at local levels to see that both parties represent their members. This can never happen unless the union itself operates democratically.

Much of my view will seem pessimistic, but I am not discouraged. Despite the long struggle for unions, they are still a fairly new feature of the American scene. Every four years, often every two years, labor becomes involved in national, state and local elections. It is still true that the lower echelons of the economic army stay away from the polls in larger numbers than their more favored brethren. This is a result of bad education and poverty. Both these conditions are correctable; to some extent they are being corrected, but more can be done. If oratory will not get the vote out, action will. Organization, preparation of lists, doorbell-ringing—in short, personal contact—will make democracy work. And in doing this, labor itself learns better citizenship.

12. Becoming an Organization Man

He who hopes to influence the direction and destiny of the labor movement must become a member in the ranks. Contrary to what one would expect from their size, unions have few jobs for trained lawyers, economists and statisticians. And their research and educational programs are not expanding rapidly. There are many reasons for this.

First, labor leaders prefer surpluses to deficits, and new or expanded programs upset the financial status quo. In this area, labor leaders are conservative and not easily moved to spend money on the new and untried. Furthermore, the costs of daily operation plus the constant pressure to maintain and expand the organization consume most of the current income. Many national and international unions are spending to the limit of their capacity while the locals are building up the reserve.

Second, the labor movement is a profoundly political movement, a movement of men who are on top and men who want to get to the top, a movement comprised of constantly conflicting ambitions. Consequently, the new employee in the labor movement is not simply a new man: he is an addition to the prestige and influence of a political leader or a department head. Because it is a question of a leader's power, it takes much longer to create a new position than to find and hire the right person. This is a fact which the novice seldom understands. All he sees is a job which needs doing and a man capable of doing it.

The best way for a newcomer to get a job is to become acquainted with the individuals in the union who are in a position to hire him. He should cultivate that acquaintance, but not so aggressively that he becomes a nuisance. The ideal means to accomplish this is by volunteering his services to the union office

73

and to the person he wants to work for—as an organizer, in political action, or even for some of the routine clerical work on which most union offices never quite catch up. By such service, he can accomplish several ends at once. He can become familiar with the staff without earning the reputation of a pest. He can gain some knowledge of the internal character of the union and some experience in its methods of work, its personalities and its intra-office politics. Most important, he can prove himself a person who is willing to work and able to execute a job successfully. When there is an opening, weeks or even months later, he will stand a good chance of getting the job.

Perhaps I can best illustrate this point from my own experience. In 1933-1934, as a teacher in the Ann Arbor, Michigan, public schools, I became interested in the Teachers Union (AFL), helped organize our local chapter and became active in its politics on both the local and the state level. Although I did not realize it then, this was the preparation for my job as executive secretary of the Chicago Teachers Union. I doubt, however, that I would have obtained that job, even with this experience, had I not met an influential and active unionist by helping her with a Teachers Union program on the University of Chicago campus. She sponsored my candidacy, and, thanks to her contact and political power, I got the job.

In 1935-1936, I spent all my spare time helping the automobile workers—organizing, speaking to middle-class groups, interpreting the union's views and representing the union in the state legislature. Again I was preparing myself by meeting the men and women who later became my bosses and coworkers. At about the same time, Raymond Walsh, a teacher at Harvard, was studying the CIO and writing its early history. Ray also was a member of the Teachers Union, and when he was under fire at Harvard for his friendliness to labor, I served as a member of his defense counsel. Consequently, we became professionally and personally acquainted. In 1940, Ray was hired by the national CIO. Some six months later, he hired me. The combination of experience and participation had again brought success.

Today the structure of the labor movement has changed. When I first worked for it, it was a fluid organization; now it is an institution with an intrenched bureaucracy at all levels. Then it was easy for volunteers to find a place within the movement; now it is not. Because of this change, men and women who wish to become a part of labor's staff should give careful attention to the particular field in which they wish to work.

If one is interested in power, prestige and a salary several times greater than fellow staff men in comparable positions within the hierarchy, then he should by all means study law. Lawyers hold exalted positions in the labor movement. They are the high priests of power, initiated in the mysteries of interpreting the law and contracts. Their chief responsibility is to tell the boss what he can and cannot do. Consequently, they acquire the privilege of speaking for him. They soon discover where the corpses of compromise are buried. Then they cannot be fired: they know too much.

Research economists are the next most important men on the union staff. They deal with all the mysteries of living costs, indexes of the Bureau of Labor Statistics and profits before and after taxes. They too are developing a cult and perhaps, in a few hundred years, will be as exalted as lawyers. Now, however, they only prepare the arguments for the contracts; the lawyers negotiate.

Public relations offers an exciting field for those hardworking extroverts who believe in what they are selling and like to work somewhere between crisis and catastrophe. As ours quickly becomes an age of public relations, press, television and mailing lists, more and more union battles are fought in public. Unions, like corporations, need their spokesmen. While some individuals may specialize directly in public relations, a command of the spoken and written word is important for everyone who wishes to make his influence felt in labor's ranks. The labor leader is almost always an able public speaker; in fact, he has often risen to the top primarily because he knows how to capture and hold an audience. The neophyte must learn to speak per-

suasively on his feet without notes. He must use the vernacular
of the workers. There is only one real way to learn how to move
an audience, and that is to speak wherever and whenever an opportunity arises. Public speaking can be learned, though sometimes it seems as much an art as a discipline.

There ought to be a course which provides practice in writing speeches, radio scripts and even eulogies and obituaries. It is
always easier to find trained economists than good writers. Even
within my classes at the university, I was discouraged when I
looked for writers capable of clear and forceful expression. My
students' papers were usually accretions and assimilations of information, not dynamic documents. Aspirants to jobs in the labor
movement should learn to think, speak, and write logically and
with conviction.

If one is inclined to question the long-range effectiveness of
the mass media, worker education sometimes offers a healthier
field. Here, however, one is faced with the fact that many union
leaders are suspicious of education: after all, ideas are dangerous,
and education may make a man more ambitious. Furthermore, it
has never been established that the educator makes a significant
contribution toward lengthening the checkoff list.

Finally, among the aristocrats of the labor movement is the
legislative expert or trained lobbyist. His chief job is to win
friends and influence legislation. In the process he meets the great
of the earth and discovers that they too are men as he is a man.
Such a discovery takes on major significance, for labor men who
move into close contact with the great must still remain uncor-
rupted by the glamour of office and power.

Although special skills are in demand in the complex labor
organization today, no amount of factual information or technical
competence is significant unless the expert knows how to use it to
advance the organization. Lawyers need to know more about life
and less about contracts; economists more about society and less
about immutable economic law. Learning is much more easily
acquired than is the wisdom to know how to apply it—an observa-
tion as old as King Solomon. The labor movement needs men

who are sensitive and alert to the life about them, not the research Ph.D. who, lacking this quality, is unhappy when his job broadens from that of counting milk bottles left on workers' doorsteps to the over-all struggle for milk.

Until unions are much better staffed, there will be little original research in the labor movement. Like many other organizations, labor is dependent upon government agencies for its basic statistical information. It is very important for an expert to know where information can be obtained, for using available research results is much more frequently his task than doing the research itself. To become proficient in his job, he must become an operator, a man who has contacts in the Bureau of Labor Statistics, the Bureau of the Census, the Departments of Commerce and Agriculture—everywhere where the busy introverts known as researchers are assembling facts and figures, useful and irrelevant.

The goal of a more equitable share of the national income for the worker is a fixed star on the union horizon. As a generally accepted point of departure, it gives the expert a clear field within which to maneuver: any facts which do not contribute to this goal are irrelevant. The expert is not an objective scientist interested in truth for its own sake; the labor movement is not a place for pure objectivity. Its work must contribute to its members' welfare. The expert must know where the facts are and how to use them to advance his organization's purposes.

Every novice must learn to accommodate himself to the policy of the organization and decide if he prefers to play an active or a passive role within it. Those who remain passive live longer. They accept the policy laid down by convention and the executive board. Usually they offer no comments unless a superior asks them for an opinion or a memorandum. Above all, they eschew working through friendly political officers to advance their interpretations of policy, lest their superiors suspect them of disloyalty. On the other hand, the activist has his own ideas about what the organization should be doing and how it should be done. He does not wait; he acts. When the boss comes to town, he puts forward a memorandum and requests an interview. During the in-

terview, he uses reasonable efforts at argument and persuasion to
influence the boss to act or not to act. Sometimes he even plants
memoranda or resolutions through friendly officers.

In the early days of the CIO and the Teachers Union, the
activists, the men with a mission, dominated the staff. Now they
have left, leaving the field to those who can accommodate themselves more easily to the status quo. I would not venture to say
which group is better; it sometimes takes more courage to stay
than it does to leave.

The novice needs friendly advice from someone who will
introduce him to the conflicts of power and personality that exist
in every organization. In my last years in the CIO, when I hired
new members for my staff, I spent hours with them, depicting the
world they had entered. Then, if they were expected to perform
tasks which had an impact on policy, I would give them a month
or six weeks simply to read resolutions, minutes and other relevant materials, as well as to get acquainted with their fellow workers during lunch hours, committee meetings and conventions.

Policy is influenced in little ways as well as great—through
ghost written speeches, memos for broadcast and innumerable articles and statements that staff men are constantly called on to
prepare. This is particularly true when one's superior officer insists on understanding the statements he signs and the speeches
he gives. In his efforts to assimilate the ideas and facts given him
by the staff man, he considers them thoroughly—and often makes
them his own. The great ideas and plans of a labor movement do
not spring up full blown.

In the CIO and to a lesser degree in the Teachers Union,
the opportunity to handle assignments for the boss is determined
by his secretary. So is the order in which the boss receives staff
memos and the ease with which one can get in to see him. Personal secretaries are their bosses' eyes and ears; when the bosses
are out of town, the secretaries are busy collecting news for their
edification on their return.

About a year after I was employed by the CIO, Ray Walsh,
my supervisor in the Department of Education and Research,

went to work for Sidney Hillman in CIO-PAC. This left me in charge of the department. Consequently, I found myself writing the statements and doing the assignments for Philip Murray that Ray had been doing. As the time passed, Murray's secretary depended on me more and more, and doubtless mentioned to Murray that I was doing the jobs. Later, when Ray left the CIO permanently, Murray was advised by his secretary to make me department head. I was available and had been approved by the eyes and ears of the boss. I was given the post without having requested it.

In the Teachers Union, the situation was somewhat different. There were actually two heads—the president and the executive secretary. In the struggle between them for control of the union, the secretaries were, of course, officially neutral. But their neutrality did not prevent them from turning the tide by offering a word here and a bit of information there. The moral is obvious: the wise expert in an organization is fortunate indeed if the secretaries are favorable to him. He must always remember that they respond to men who know that not all the brains are in the higher echelons.

Every organization has two main components, the constitutional and the informal. American presidents have cabinets; and if the historians are right, they are also influenced by their companions at poker. The same situation exists in the labor movement. Most of the leaders of labor come up through the ranks. They live their lives in conflict, and the loyalty and the courage of their companions are vital to them. Furthermore, these relationships are established in the years before the leader becomes a national figure. Those who have lived, fought and sometimes starved together are bound by ties which few newcomers can break through. It is important for the young expert who goes into the labor movement to understand these affinities and to realize how important they are. He must understand that he will never quite be a part of this inner fellowship.

This is a hard lesson to learn, and one which I never completely grasped. It was difficult for me to accept the fact that I was an outsider in a group which commended my utmost loyalties and for which I had taken risks and made sacrifices. My background was different. I was a wealthy farmer's son; they were workers. I had never really been economically insecure; they had gone hungry. I had gone to school; they had not. I had grown up in a Puritan, temperate tradition; they had not. For me there was another world outside the labor movement; for them, labor was the only world. Doubtless the present generation of college-trained, middle-class neophytes are undergoing similar soul searching experiences. Although the beginner can never become a member of the inner circle, he must with all his strength resist the temptation to flee this frustrating situation. The ways of running away are many. The chief reason for the existence of both the AFL and the CIO was to organize the unorganized and to improve the welfare of the organized. Theoretically, all the efforts and activities of the AFL and the CIO were focused upon these aims. Staff men were expected to understand this, and a director of research and education doubly so. Specifically, the primary responsibility of the director of research and education was to serve as a resource man in the economic and legislative struggle which depended upon data on wages, taxes, and other economic facts. After he had finished this primary job, he might give attention to education. But the expert may prefer to educate rather than perform the grinding work of research, especially when the aims of research are dictated. He is often tempted to neglect his main job for that which he likes best.

There are also many worthy yet diverting auxiliary interests. Consequently, there is a constant temptation to be absent when the president and the executive board meet. But it is precisely at these times that the opportunity occurs to become a real part of the labor movement. The newcomer must stick to the main channel and do his best to become a part of the operational units. If he is away too often, there may be no desk for him when he returns. More seriously, the boss may have turned over his assignment to someone else, and the contacts he coveted will be gone forever.

This does not mean, of course, that the expert need sacrifice himself, body and soul, to the organization. Nor does it mean that compromise becomes a virtue above all others. It does mean that the expert must become a man capable of bending but not breaking. Above all, he must be able to understand all the complex gears which must mesh before the machine can go forward. Becoming an organization man is no easy task, particularly for the intellectual. There are few vicarious ways to learn the art. But it is an art which must be learned in a society whose destiny is more and more determined by organizations. Those who would serve must be an integral part of the process in which serving and learning take place.

13. Kept Men

Practically everyone I know has a favorite candidate for the title of "greatest threat to democracy and democratic institutions." To some, it is reaction carried to the ultimate; to others, communism; to yet others, socialism, the supposed stepping stone to communism. To liberals the threat is most often laissez faire, the indifference of those whose feet are mired in the status quo.

Most of my friends see democracy threatened from the right by the power wielded by great wealth and giant corporations. Instinctively I share these apprehensions; yet my greatest fear for free institutions centers not on those who are powerful, but on the ever-increasing numbers of kept men—men who are the prisoners of an ideology, an institution or an organization. When these men speak, they do not voice a free and self-determined opinion; they merely mouth the official apologies for policies external to their own beliefs.

The prevalence of kept men has spread a poisonous suspicion throughout our society. For years I worked for the labor movement and was an advocate of organized labor's point of view. Several years have passed since I left my position with organized labor, yet to the world I remain stereotyped as a special pleader despite the fact that even when I was on labor's payroll, I prided myself on my independence.

For well over a decade, I have been a member of the Federal and now the National Council of Churches' Commission on Church and Economic Life. In recent years our task has been to reconcile Christian ethics and economic practices. At these meetings, I am constantly struck by the persistence with which each special-interest group reiterates its point of view. There are spokesmen for labor, for business, for the cooperatives. Agriculture's representatives speak not only for that bloc but for its separate pieces—the bureau, the grange, the union. As a result, more often than not we plunge from discussion into debate. Papers are debated from the bias of the special interests; resolutions are reached only when the uncommitted, usually ministers or educators, align themselves with one static point of view or another.

How would it be possible to get more discussion and less debate? Discussion, I am convinced, would allow a real airing of the problems. The spokesmen's "off the record" feelings are much more amenable to compromise, and so to better resolutions.

Recently, I had an experience which both pained and shocked me—probably because I had known the men involved for many years and had learned to respect their integrity. The incident issued from my doubt about the bona fide motive of a strike, a doubt shared by some of the most competent reporters. I asked two union friends their opinion. For more than half an hour they gave me the official interpretation of the union's case including the charge that the industry had failed to bargain in good faith. Then one of my friends left, and the other, who remained alone with me, said confidentially, "Do you realize that [the union president] held up the research staff reports on the ability of the industry to pay, and the productivity studies, until it was too late for them to have any effect on public opinion? Why do you suppose he did that if he and [the president of the corporation involved] didn't have an understanding?"

Of course, we will probably never know the truth. For me, it is sufficient to know that men close to the situation had their doubts and were very reluctant to express them. Their silence may have been justified, for to speak out would have meant professional suicide. One lesson that staff men in private economic organizations learn early is never publicly to disagree with or question the policy of their organization. And if they want to avoid the emotional conflicts which lead to ulcers, they had best not do much private questioning either. The safest of all attitudes is simply to take the position: "I supply the facts on which the arguments rest. What happens after that isn't my problem."

Perhaps it is the nature of economic organizations which makes such reactions almost inevitable. We achieve more and more of our economic security through group action in combination with government—local, state and federal. One result is that ours is becoming a compensatory society, one in which groups are rewarded in proportion to the power they command.

I recall how we in the CIO used to make our periodic pilgrimages to the Council of Economic Advisors to exchange opinions on the economic state of the nation. By means of the Council, we sought to exert our influence on the President, who, in turn, would exert his power on the Congress through his semi-annual messages. Of course, our spokesmen made it clear that the total economy is best served when the worker-consumer has an increasing ability to buy the products of our machines. We pointed out too that industrial profits were exorbitantly high and should be taxed more, especially since lower income individuals were already paying a disproportionate share. In short, we equated the larger good with our private good. And I still believe that, relatively speaking, we were near to the truth. But we were not unique in our thesis: every other group used similar arguments from its own vantage ground. Ultimately the argument will run its course, and the respective groups will achieve an equilibrium through check and countercheck.

I know that there are schools of thought which hold that the individual has no responsibility beyond the organization of which he is a part. After all, the reasoning goes, suppose the individual opposes his organization's position and is fired: of what use will he be then? I admit that there is much validity in this argument. Indeed, I have told more than one class that it may take more courage to stay inside an organization and make the compromise than to resign in deference to the claims of private morality.

And yet, I plead for private morality, even with the risks it involves. I know of no other way to call attention to situations that threaten the general well-being. Economic and political organizations are better served if there are individuals willing to defy the conspiracies of silence, to risk losing position and election in order to get the broader issues into the open. The question of why there are so few willing to take this risk has troubled me for a long time. Sometimes I think it is because of our attitude toward compromises. As a nation of competing organizations and conflicting pressures, we are forced to compromise in order to maintain a modicum of stability. Nor is this necessarily bad. It is perhaps the only way that all of the nation's many diversified interests can be treated fairly. One can even argue that a larger, fuller truth is occasionally revealed in the compromise through which a difficulty is resolved.

I have worked in organizations and have compromised. I continue to do so daily, and I teach my students that compromise is often necessary in a choice between conflicting principles. But I also teach them that there is a point at which a man must respect his sense of a higher morality and stand beyond compromise. This is not an easy decision to make, for to reject compromise may mean being fired or being compelled to resign. If one has children, or is past middle age or lacks the educational training or contacts to get another job, then it is no easy task to follow one's conscience and precipitate discussion. But precipitate it one must, for the only way to bring major issues into focus is to challenge the institution.

Today, the educators and professionals employed by the labor movement are, by and large, apologists for the existing leaders and the existing power structures. These people have both the knowledge and the position from which to question most intelligently the status quo, yet they are the ones who do the least questioning. They are the kept men, as are their counterparts in corporations, although we have always attributed higher motives and goals to men working with the labor movement than to those wearing gray flannel suits.

There is a simple way to identify kept men: they are unwilling to study the impact of their power world on the rank and file membership and on themselves. They are always more willing to study power in someone else's bailiwick. This also holds true in universities. Here the best studies are made of the power of unions, political parties and governments—but to the best of my knowledge, no good studies of politics and power relationships in the universities themselves. The only significant way to understand power is to know, from direct experience, where it pinches. Kept men can feel the pinch, but they are not apt to make objective studies of it.

Kept men are constantly being called on to do right things for the wrong reasons—plead for racial integration, for example, because (1) to the colored peoples of the world, our racial intolerance casts doubts on our diplomatic positions; (2) Communists take advantage of our racist policies to agitate against us; and (3) in case of war, we would certainly need the loyalty of our colored brethren. Or we are asked to plead that inflation is a threat. But why should one union assume a responsibility? Isn't productivity increasing? Aren't profits the highest ever? Or we are called upon to plead that management is being pressured by the union. But how can one corporation stem the inflation tide?

The illustrations around us are endless. In a sense, we are all kept men. I would not mind this so much if the wrong reasons were at least our own. But they are not: they are the rationales of the group or groups with which we identify. I believe that if men would stop and examine these questions—examine them as men, not as union staff men or corporation executives—they would soon act for the right reasons, for their own reasons.

14. Study Them Alive

While I was working for organized labor, my ideas were often solicited by students who were studying the labor movement. Heaven alone knows how many questionnaires I filled out—enough, certainly, to have developed a profound skepticism of their efficiency as tools for understanding the labor movement and its leaders. Now I am a teacher and more busy than ever trying to help students who are interested in organized labor.

I have never failed to be impressed by my initial interviews with students about to embark on a piece of labor research. Characteristically, the individual is eager with questions, eager with a desire to know and understand the dynamics of labor. But too often I find that this same student expects to satisfy his thirst by spending conscientious hours with the files of union offices and by analyzing the results of long and detailed questionnaires.

Students who come to labor unions expecting to find an endless file of confidential and revealing documents are usually disappointed. In the first place, there are few such files and documents. This is a technological era; the epistolary art is dead. Things once negotiated in writing are now settled over the telephone, and very seldom is there a secretary taking down the words. Nor are the significant statements of the big brass in their political huddles recorded. Theirs are usually gentlemen's agreements, arrived at within the framework of existing forces and balances. Furthermore, the labor movement is not too far removed from the days of the Pinkerton raids and company stooges; and men who have had their files raided are not too anxious to establish intimate records. Nor are the labor leaders concerned about the vacuum they create for future historians when they fail to put their more significant conversations and agreements into writing.

Even the files are not permanent: those filled with papers of secondary importance are thrown away at regular intervals. For example, all of Sidney Hillman's accumulated records and much of his correspondence were consigned to the waste basket after his death.

The situation is not as serious as one might suppose, however. I have written and ghost written several thousand memos over the years, and I can safely say none of them are written to facilitate the writing of theses. They are written to interpret events at a meeting in such a way as to give direction to the next meeting or, conversely, to reverse the direction projected at the last meeting. All memos are political, written in a political environment for political reasons. They are written for the record and can only be interpreted if that record and the persons involved in it are understood.

I brought with me to the University of Chicago the memos I wrote while in the CIO. Occasionally I look at them and dream about a book which might be written on power and policy formation in the labor movements. More often, however, I recall the meetings from which the memos grew: the people present, the relaxed or heated exchanges, the jockeying for position in the power structure, all the interplays which become discernible only when one knows the balances between men and events. Memory alone can provide the real meaning to those memos describing the efforts to bring about labor unity, or to those recounting the day Allan Haywood came into Philip Murray's office while I was pleading for an expanded budget and asked how many dues-paying members educators brought into CIO. Should I use these memos, they would only be pegs on which to hang all the unwritten impressions and happenings.

Memos vary according to the purposes of the men who write them. It was often my delightful experience to go through the jockeying necessary to get a memo on some economically significant issue placed on the desk of one of the bosses. Other men motivated by other ideologies and ambitions did likewise. Consequently, each of our bosses, like all good politicians, had expert comment on the others' work. In the process, victories or defeats were registered vis-à-vis the power structure.

Men who feel deeply fight hard and are apt to record in their files their original memos or the amended versions which reflect their point of view. As a researcher, I would want to see both the Jim Carey and the Lee Pressman versions of any CIO event. For these were aggressive personalities, motivated by definite power drives which were related to different philosophies of history. They hated each other with a hatred that bordered on the magnificent.

Every organization has its official documents, and the labor movement is no exception. One of the most important is the *Convention Report and Resolutions* which usually includes the president's report, the reports of the various staff people and the reports of constitutional or standing committees. These reports, plus a foreword by the president, give an over-all account of the administration stewardship. But here again, the student-researcher must remember that these documents, no less than the memos, are a political medium.

Naturally, each department head or committee chairman is conscious of the motive of his report. Each realizes that his department or committee will be justified by it. He tries to make both himself and the administration look good, and incidentally argues for the continuation of his department or committee. But while the relation of the staff to the administration helps shape these reports, they are also influenced by the ambitions and political orientation of each department head or committee chairman.

Convention reports are a little more spontaneous. It is not so easy to control delegates. However, as more and more labor organizations are engulfed by bureaucrats, the same problems rise to the surface. Speeches at labor meetings are controlled by the presiding chairman through his recognition of speakers. The same is often true of demonstrations and applause.

A resolution which purports to express the will of the membership and which would guide the organization for the following year may be a genuine product of the rank-and-file delegates from some local. On the other hand, it may be drawn up by a staff man and planted in the local delegation. Or, if the staff man does not wish to follow the resolution through the long grinding of the union machinery, he may turn it over indirectly to the secretary of the resolutions committee and begin the nursing process with friendly members of that committee.

Really important resolutions, such as those dealing with wages, communism or foreign policy, are the results of staff action rather than rank-and-file agitation. They are prepared at the order of the big brass, approved by them and usually agreed upon before they are put into the hopper. When the resolutions come before the convention, the officers speak for them in direct order of rank in the union hierarchy, and they are usually passed unanimously. Lesser resolutions, such as those supporting a labor extension bill, are passed mechanically, and long speeches supporting them are frowned upon. But the final report of the convention does not indicate the process by which the resolutions were adopted. Such information does not come ready packaged for the student. He must search for it by getting as close to the process as he possibly can.

Much more might be said about these reports and about the resolutions which grow out of the convention. But enough has been said to make it perfectly clear that they are not created in a vacuum, that even the president's report is caught in the cross-currents of personal and political differences. Nevertheless, these reports and resolutions are the most adequate sources for obtaining a picture of union activity, with the possible exception of official minutes. While I was with the Chicago Teachers Union, all executive board and House of Representative meetings were recorded by a competent office secretary as well as by the recording secretary. Occasionally there were discrepancies due to the bias of the recording secretary, who was, after all, a political official. Much the same practice prevails in the AFL-CIO. The main motions are recorded by the secretary-treasurer at executive board meetings, but the stenographic reports are used as the basis for the secretary's reports of these meetings. At the national convention and other large meetings, the records are taken down by court reporters or stenotypists.

Without the original transcripts, the struggles of an organization are difficult to understand and describe. I have not heard of a single student able to gain access to the official minutes of the CIO executive board meetings or of any of its internationals. Only time will make them available. Studies of the daily workings of the union are much less difficult to obtain; the records of the press, checked against the union reports, make a fairly complete story possible. The reason is obvious: internal political power struggles are covered up, but not the struggles for economic gains. One has only to imagine the resistance a researcher would encounter studying the personnel practices of unions, in contrast to the cooperation he would give in a study of the personnel practices of industry.

The files of union offices are filled with pamphlets describing the union's economic and social programs. These pamphlets were all written with two objectives in mind: to activate the rank and file and to woo the public to the union's point of view, always identifying the union's interest with the public interest.

Some of the finest and most objective presentations in all union literature are contained in the testimonies before congressional committees. The pattern is simple: the introductory statement contains the position of the union, and the argument confirms it. Hence, there is little room for evasion or circumlocution. If there is circumlocution, it comes in the interpretations given those speeches and testimonies in the labor press. There are no objective labor papers. Most of them are puff sheets, dedicated to praising the boss and maintaining the status quo.

Such are the documentary sources for research on unions. Let me now pay my respects to the questionnaire, particularly to the mailed questionnaire. As a source of understanding the union movement and union personalities, it is even more deceptive than misunderstood documents.

In the first place, a busy union official has no time to fill them out. He sends them to an assistant, who theoretically determines which staff man is most competent to fill them out and passes them on to him. If the staff man is busy, *he* sends the papers along to one of his own assistants. Usually they are then presented to the staff man's assistant's secretary, who hasn't anyone to pass them on to.

As educational officer in both the labor organizations in which I served, I seemed to get more than my share of questionnaires. The political officers who passed them on to me must have felt that a union educator is a little less pragmatic than other union people and so might be more inclined to fill out the blanks. Besides, an educator's time is less valuable than that of a lawyer fighting Taft-Hartley or a busy researcher working on a wage case.

The largest number of questionnaires ever to come to my desk at once was eleven. I filled out nine; then, incapable of devising any new variations, I had my secretary fill out the last two. I understand that these last replies are included in C. Wright Mills' *The New Men of Power.*

Lest this seem too cynical, let me add that not all questionnaires are handled this cavalierly. There were times when I knew the person who sent them, or when the cover letter or contents of the questionnaire stimulated my interest. These naturally received more than perfunctory replies. But the fact still remains that there is no department or person within the labor movement whose chief task it is to see that questionnaires are properly and equitably handled.

I wish every person who sent or contemplates sending a questionnaire to a union official or one of his staff men could see the stack of mail which comes daily to such a man's desk and understand that matters of immediate concern to the union come first. (Philip Murray used to read the badly scrawled personal letters from steel workers before anything else on his desk.) Most union leaders are activists by temperament and not suited to the minutiae of desk work.

Of course, not all questionnaires are directed to the top brass. Some go to the lower executive and staff levels, some to the rank and file. Naturally, the likelihood of getting a well-studied reply from an officer on the lower levels is much greater.

My dissatisfaction with questionnaires goes beyond methodology. Too often they are designed to ascertain the obvious or to prove the already agreed upon. Indeed, I am more inclined to trust the insights of a novelist than the measurements of a statistician.

These limitations in the traditional methods of labor research will not, I hope, discourage such research. We are achieving a new political equilibrium in which labor will inevitably play an increasingly significant part. As Merlyn Pitzele said so clearly in an article in *Labor and Nation* (Spring 1950), "Union politics do not stop at the union's edge. They are public politics as well." But the motive of these politics can only be understood by people who participate in them. We need to find and develop men in labor's own ranks who, as participant observers, are conscious of the history they are making and are willing to write about it.

Perhaps I am trying to reconcile the age-old dilemma that men who make history seldom write it and those who write it seldom make it. But if the dilemma cannot be reconciled, we can at least advise students to go into the movement, become a part of it and get close enough to its history to get the feel of its dynamics. We can urge students to work with, work for—even live with— the boss, and take down his reminiscences in the moments he is relaxed. Or the clinics could gather the available information relative to any event and then check it with the history maker on the understanding that anything he said would be kept confidential until a reasonable period after his death.

This is the kind of history which puts flesh on the bones of fact. When I first came to the Chicago Teachers Union and began to handle their negotiations, I was thrown into constant contact with John Fitzpatrick, the old AFL pioneer. Occasionally he would be in a talkative mood, and the insights he gave me on AFL politics and personalities transcended anything I ever read in books. For years I have spent hours quizzing men like John Brophy of the CIO about John L. Lewis. Brophy knows Lewis and the miners better than any other man alive, and no record exists of his knowledge outside of his life and memory. Why shouldn't a student live with a man like John Brophy, write his biography, bring together the history which his life encompassed and then speculate how different the miners would be today if Brophy, rather than Lewis, had been their leader.

Clearly, a relationship which can lead to an honest exchange of thought is not built overnight. Most labor leaders who come up from the ranks distrust intellectuals. They are not sure they can be trusted when the chips are down, when it is necessary to hit the bricks. The student who undertakes an extensive research project in the field of labor and industrial relations must learn to appreciate the reality of the factory world: the smell of grease and oil and sweat, the lunch basket, the sound of factory noise, the compulsion of the assembly line, the ride at midnight on a crowded bus with fellow workers. He must learn to regard workers as people, not as concepts in an economic theory.

Experience on the assembly line is valuable, for this is the real and vital area of conflict confronting union organization. But the student must also find other perspectives: conferences in the smoke-filled rooms, discussions with men over a glass of beer after a union meeting or standing in the picket line during a strike, conversation at conventions with members of other locals. Such discussion and participation focuses the student's attention on problems as they exist and orients him realistically to the union situation.

It is out of such experiences and relationships that men mold their souls and it is in such experiences and relationships that they bare them. While I did not share all of the struggles of the auto workers, I did bore holes in the running boards at Studebaker. I know how it feels to be tied to a machine, and I did help organize in Michigan when we were afraid to meet in homes. I went through the Flint sit-down days, helped peel potatoes and crank mimeographs, spoke in rooms filled with company goons and had a teacher contract held up because of my union work. I made friends with men who were willing to die so that their children would know a better world. It takes time and several beers to bring a life into focus.

15. The Wirepullers

The attempts of unions and employers to influence and control the opinion of our citizens take place within the framework of a compensatory state—that is, a state in which economic groups compete for government favors, and in which our government grants or withholds its favors with an eye to staying in power. This is not a particularly new phenomenon. From the very beginning of our republic, economic groups have struggled for the favors of the state. The significant new factors are the increasing size and power of the competing groups and the presence of organized labor as one of the more powerful of these groups.

The working of this compensatory process is illustrated by the way in which the President's Council of Economic Advisors functions. Before preparing its annual report on the economic health of the nation, the council hears the evidence of the great economic pressure groups: labor, agriculture and business. Occasionally even small business and consumer groups present their cases. Representatives of these interests appear before the council and its staff to present their arguments for or against wage increases without price increases, for or against continuing subsidies for agriculture and for or against the existing or proposed corporation taxes.

The council hears the special pleaders, makes its own investigation of the facts and then writes its report, which it transmits to the President. The President uses the material in the report as a basis for his message to Congress. But the President's message is an adaptation of the report, and his adaptation is determined not only by his responsibilities as President of the United States but also by his role as leader of the political party in power. In this latter role, he must try to hold the loyalties of the groups which support him and his party; in this message, as in others, he projects his party's program.

Similarly, the Taft-Hartley Act exemplifies an issue on which unions and employers have sought to influence public opinion and government action in their behalf. Employers have represented it as a bill to free labor, to preserve the worker's right of individual choice. Organized labor has fought it as a bill to enslave labor. Its enactment represented a triumph in Congress for its supporters, but not necessarily a final triumph. Both groups are still hard at work convincing the public that it is a good or a bad piece of legislation. Both national parties have given it recognition as an issue in their platforms. Candidates find it necessary to take positions on the issue, and each takes what he hopes will be the most popular. His position, he argues, is the one most consistent with the public interest.

This identification of the special group's interest with the public interest is characteristic of the campaigns of all groups which seek to influence public opinion. The differences among business, labor and agriculture appear in their contrasting definitions of the public interest and their different notions about how it is best advanced. Organized labor believes that it is in the public interest to raise the standard of living for all. It would achieve this by increasing the purchasing power of organized workers and by organizing the unorganized so that they may have similar privileges. They believe there is much to be done so long as income is distributed in such a way that the lowest 20 per cent of income recipients in America receive 5 per cent of the total money income whereas the upper 20 per cent receive 45 per cent (1953 statistics).

Other pressure groups define the public interest and its advancement differently. The farmer argues that agriculture is the backbone of the nation: "How could we get along without food and fibre?" Business insists that the nation's economic strength is dependent on the constant creation of jobs and that this requires a constant expansion of capital investment, which must not be drained off by excessive taxes.

Each group is sincere, and each follows a similar routine in attempting to influence public opinion and legislation. At all political levels—local, state or national—three major methods are used to promote the interests of the special group: lobbying, mass media and education.

Lobbying activities take several forms. Most commonly, they provide a channel for communicating public opinion and the opinions of special groups to legislators. By contacting congressmen and appearing before legislative committees, the lobbyist supplies information pertinent to the interest of the group he represents. Frequently, much of the substantive information on bills introduced and passed by national and state legislatures is provided by organizations which sponsor the legislation. In fact, bills are often drafted by the lobbyist and then introduced by a legislator who is friendly to the special interest group.

A second type of lobbying stresses the reaction of voters and focuses the legislator's attention on the support he will gain or lose by his stand. The third—and most destructive—type is the fix and the squeeze. What begins as wining and dining to set an atmosphere for discussion has been known to turn into outright bribery.

Both unions and employers make use of mass media—the press, radio, television, films, pamphlets, comic strips, etc.—but generally in a manipulative way. The typical full-page ad concentrates more on dramatic design and loaded words than on facts. It is designed to sell, not to inform.

The third method of influencing public and legislative opinion presupposes that individuals are capable of thinking for themselves. It aims at giving people the facts and encouraging them to consider issues. It seeks to inform rather than to impress. Such education cannot be mechanical; it demands a person-to-person relationship between those teaching and those taught. It requires an opportunity to question and to disagree. Ideas cannot be sold. They are the outgrowth of discussion and reading, based on respect for the other person's point of view.

In the days of relatively full employment, labor disputes call forth some rather unusual appeals to the public. The employer appeals to the public as consumers; he argues that wage increases would hurt the consumers through price increases. The union replies that the employer's profits are enormous and that he could easily pay the wage increases without raising prices. When the government intervenes in a labor dispute and either party objects to the government's action, the public is urged to throw the rascals out.

In elections, organized labor appeals for support for those candidates whose records or campaign promises make them seem friends of labor. As friends of labor, they are assumed to be friends of the public. Employer groups, of course, never appeal for support of their candidates as friends of employers. These candidates, even when hostile to organized labor, are also presented as friends of labor, believers in free enterprise and the American way of life.

Organized labor has developed a comprehensive understanding of economic cause and effect, and this in turn has increased its interest in politics. The top labor leaders and their intellectual advisers understand that the CIO grew up with Roosevelt, Article 7A of the National Reconstruction Act and the Wagner Act, and that the AFL doubled its membership under the same friendly aegis. The walls which have shored up the workers' security—minimum wage, unemployment insurance, old age and survivors' insurance—are the walls of legislation.

The conditions under which collective bargaining takes place are created not only by legislation but by administrative action as well. In recent years, contract negotiations have involved constant study of the cost of living. Arguments have developed between unions and employers regarding the alleged biases of the Bureau of Labor Statistics index, which measures changes in the cost of living. When changes in wage rates hinge on changes in the cost-of-living index, labor is concerned that inflationary increases not be understated. Its distrust stems from its feeling that the bureau's statisticians may be too dependent upon business sources for their facts. Under other circumstances, employers might well charge bias in the other direction.

The experts, politicians and intelligentsia in the labor movement understand that an increasing number of decisions are made at the top governmental levels in our compensatory state. They also understand the nature of the American two-party system, in which conflicting economic groups struggle for control of the parties and candidates, reconcile their conflicts around a common denominator of interests and compete with their opponents for fulfillment of their aims.

Organized labor seeks to operate politically in much the same manner as other organized interest groups. It is seldom so revolutionary that it wishes to change the established economic system or the current rules of the political organization. Its ambition, instead, is to achieve ever increasing security for its members within the existing political and economic structure.

Despite their mutual conflict, employers and unions are both anxious to secure the public's good will. Neither can afford to lose customers for the products they join to create, and unions cannot afford to stir up popular ill will if they wish to elect candidates who will protect and support their interests.

In their efforts to influence public opinion and action, both groups use the same machinery. Some of this machinery, however, lends itself more readily to use by one group than by the other.

Both labor and management participate in lobbying in its most constructive form. Both groups reach legislators and appear before legislative committees to give information on pending bills. There is an increasing representation of labor in committee hearings, and labor now comes supplied with its own lawyers, economists and statisticians to match the experts who testify for business groups.

The second type of lobbying, that which stresses the giving or withholding of support for a legislator, depending on his vote, is carried on differently by the two groups. Organized labor rates senators and representatives by their voting records in committees and in roll call votes on so-called labor bills. If a legislator fails to measure up to expectations, he is threatened with the withdrawal of support by labor's voting bloc. In reality, organized labor does not vote as a bloc; the leaders may influence its vote, but they by no means control it. In addition, while almost one-fourth of all families in America are labor union families, union members maintain a distinctly low voter turnout. Nevertheless, unions do organize political action committees, and they do work to get out the vote. They represent a formidable number of voters, and their strength cannot be dismissed lightly.

Employers and business groups can point to no such voting group, but they do have an advantage which not even a united labor organization can match. They can offer or withhold another kind of support. The great game of politics in the United States is an expensive one, and it is here that big money talks.

The fix and the squeeze, which are characteristic of the third and most destructive type of lobbying, also require sizable expenditures. More and more individuals and organizations look to the government to help them engineer economic advantage through grants-in-aid, government contracts, price supports, tax exemptions and the like. In the confusion which is Capitol Hill, the uninitiated seek the help of the initiated, and money and liquor flow to bridge the gaps of justice and reason. This kind of political activity undermines public morals and destroys public confidence.

Both the venal and the unsophisticated live in a world of influence. Both agree that the only way to get things done in Washington is through someone else. And to persuade someone else to act may require a subtle kind of bribery or special pressure. The danger of such a philosophy is that the fix and the squeeze may become so firmly institutionalized in our culture, as they have in China, that they will threaten the very basis of our democratic processes.

In the last analysis, the integrity of the law and the stability of our institutions are dependent on the integrity of the men who administer them. But when pressure groups have avowedly materialistic motives and when they can spend money in quantities, bribery provides a relatively easy means for achieving their goals. The moral patterns of a society which produced the fix and the squeeze are affecting the political strategy of increasing numbers of groups. Wining and dining are accepted; expensive gifts may be condemned in political speeches, but they are all too often winked at in private. Even men who represent organized labor today believe that, to be effective, they, too, must operate through cocktail parties and large expense accounts.

The fact that the employers have more money than labor does give them a decided advantage in employing the mass media. Full page ads and radio speeches by company executives are standard operating procedure for business when a strike is in progress. But they are expensive procedures, and those who pay the bills in the labor movement know that they cannot compete with the great business organizations in such media. Although the public service responsibility of radio and television stations requires that they give time for the discussion of public issues, often that time is allotted in off-hours when listeners are few. Furthermore, the purchase of too much space and time by unions to tell their story may boomerang. The public may ask how, if the workers are as hard-pressed as they claim, their unions can afford such vast expenditures for TV time and ads.

There are other important reasons why the mass media lend themselves more readily to use by employer groups than by organized labor. Employer groups have no large membership base to which they can appeal for support and which in turn will reach others outside their group. They must use the mass media to reach the public, if only at a superficial level. While the public is undoubtedly influenced to some extent, there is good reason to believe that mass appeal often falls flat. From 1936 to 1940, for example, 90 to 95 per cent of the American press opposed Franklin Roosevelt. Americans are a newspaper-reading people, yet they elected Roosevelt for an unprecedented third term in 1940.

When I was with the CIO and CIO-PAC, I helped to develop its public relations program, following the precedents of the manipulator making use of the mass media. However, as the program was perfected, I lost faith in much that I had helped to develop. The reason was simple: I found that genuine education, through the exchange of ideas in personal relationships, repeatedly triumphed over the mass media techniques. For instance, in 1944 the CIO-PAC put out between forty and eighty million pieces of literature to help re-elect Franklin Roosevelt. The AFL put out little or no literature. Approximately 71 per cent of the registered CIO voters and about 68 per cent of the registered AFL voters voted for Roosevelt. Millions of pieces of literature—and a 3 per cent difference in the voting pattern!

Nevertheless, the temparion for unions to use the mass media is constant. And to the extent that they imitate the slick public relations of the wealthier organized interests, they neglect other means of influencing political and social direction which are more in harmony with the structure of their organizations.

It is in the third method of influencing public opinion, the more personal approach, that unions have a decided advantage. A good public relations program for the labor movement is not very different from a good educational program within the union. The worker who has confidence in his union, participates in it and knows its program is a natural interpreter of the union's point of view. Wherever he meets people, he speaks up with confidence, thus personalizing its goals. Such union members are a far more effective resource than time or space purchased in mass media for a public relations program.

Companies with a record of good labor relations have found that friendly employees are the best public relations, not only for their product but also for an atmosphere of good will toward the company in the community. The company without such a good record has, apart from its paid publicity men, only its relatively few supervisory employees and perhaps a few stockholders to tell its side of the story.

In appealing at once to their memberships and to the larger public, both union leaders and company executives are often caught in ambivalent positions. Union leaders must make a vigorous effort to secure what their members demand, yet, to gain the public's support, these demands must be reasonable. Similarly, company executives may find themselves reporting to their stockholders and investors that profits are at a record level, while at the same time resisting wage increases on grounds that profits are not adequate to cover them.

I stress this ambivalence because without it the public relations program of an organized interest group cannot be understood. Such a program is concerned as much with keeping the membership happy as with influencing public opinion. To achieve both aims, it must prove that the organization at once provides special benefits to its members and is subservient to the general public interest. In addition, both parties identify their organizational aims with human and national welfare. Business does not advertise that it is in business to make profits. Rather it "makes possible the employment of hundreds of thousands," and "provides the dependable, efficient service essential to the economic well-being and military strength of our nation." When organized labor sets up a public relations program, it, too, seeks to convince the public of its high moral purpose.

The keystone of the CIO public relations program was at one time a mailing list of some 120,000 people from all over the United States. This list was divided into fifty-two categories: teachers, ministers, political scientists, educators, reporters, radio announcers, organization heads, etc. These people received a constant flow of literature interpreting the CIO's position on various issues. In times of crisis, a statement of the reasons for the CIO's direct actions was accompanied by a personal letter that attempted to identify the CIO's interest with that of the readers. Whenever interested parties replied to the literature, their names were put on cards and classified according to states and congressional districts: this list became the nucleus of the Citizens Political Action Committee when labor went into politics full tilt in 1944.

The philosophy behind such Citizens PAC was clear cut: a faith that personal relations are more important in influencing opinion than a barrage of propaganda. Such two-way communication is not only more effective, it is more consistent with democratic institutions, which depend on a genuinely informed electorate participating in the decisions which affect them.

As the conflicting economic groups grow larger and more powerful, more and more decisions are made by top level experts and politicians. This trend will continue as long as people feel that they can do little or nothing to affect their own destiny. It is the responsibility of leaders of the conflicting groups to involve their membership in decisions, to urge their participation and to discuss all facets of the issues with them. The organizational press must do more than report. Its columns should be open to a discussion of issues; letters-to-the-editor columns should find room for all the pros and cons. Such columns exist in all too few journals of the labor and business press.

Today business, labor and agriculture are convinced that domestic inflation is almost as great a threat to the stability of American institutions as communism, yet each group is contributing in its own way to inflation. Business seeks to increase its profits, agriculture its price supports and labor its wages. Each group charges the other with causing inflation; each is willing to support the higher taxes that would control inflation—provided the taxes are levied on someone else. If the rank and file members of these same groups understood this inflationary process, if they could compare the losses they would suffer from inflation with the extra burden of taxation, there might be unprecedented agreement and pressure on Congress to raise their taxes.

Bargaining collectively in good faith more often than not resolves conflicts. In the same way, free and informed discussion may well prove the only means for competing economic groups to find harmony. To the extent that manipulative techniques and purchased influence prevail, the conflict will be aggravated, not lessened.

16. Never the Twain Shall Meet

There's lumberjacks, and teamsters, and sailors from the sea,
And there's farming boys from Texas and the hills of Tennessee;
There's miners from Kentucky, and there's fishermen from Maine;
Every worker in the country rides that Farmer-Labor Train.

Listen to the jingle, the rumble, and the roar.
She's a-rolling thru New England to the West Pacific Shore;
It's a long time we been waiting, now she's whistling round the
    bend,
Now we'll ride into the White House on the Farmer-Labor Train.

Not so long ago, when Woodie Guthrie borrowed the tune
of the "Wabash Cannonball" for his "Farmer-Labor Train" to
shout out the longings of industrial workers for farmer-labor unity,
he was celebrating an old drama and an unfulfilled wish. For the
unity did not, does not and may never exist in America.

There is every logical reason for such unity. It takes no
research in economics to show that labor represents the market
for the farmer's products. But this doesn't move the farmer.
When he goes to town to buy a cream separator and finds prices
high, he damns not his real enemy—the monopolist manufacturer
—but the wage-earner and his high wages.

The position of the labor unions in seeking farmer-labor
unity is that of the eager suitor who just can't get the girl to listen.
The mating calls go unanswered.

Lyle Cooper, research director of the United Packinghouse
Workers, once described (in an article for *The Packinghouse
Worker* entitled "Reasons for a Farmer-Labor Program") the way
many workers come to the big packing centers from the surrounding farmlands. They take jobs in the fall months when farm work
eases up. The big companies in such centers as Ottumwa and

Waterloo, Iowa, are suspected of deliberately recruiting the farm boys. "Unquestionably," Cooper wrote, "the big reason is their belief that workers with a farm background won't be much concerned about wages and conditions—that they will 'take' what the company says or does without question."

The best publicity for the union, Cooper suggested, is a converted farmer-worker who returns to his family. When "such a man or woman tells his neighbors what it's like on the killing floor, or that keeping up with a hog chain for eight hours is a bruising grind, those neighbors will believe him." This might offset the farmers' habit of blaming only the Packinghouse union every time a strike interferes with livestock marketing.

Labor already has done more than its fair share in promoting farmer-labor unity. But it is still getting much the same kind of response from farm representatives that CIO organizers received in 1936 in Hershey, Pennsylvania. The organizers went to the farmers in the section with the plea, "Don't sell your milk to the factories when the workers are on strike." The Mennonite farmers rose as one body and drove out the organizers with pitchforks.

The AFL has subsidized unions of agricultural workers, and union representatives attend county fairs. Yet about the same situation exists today as in 1948 when farmers and labor in Iowa supported the same candidate for governor. The farm representatives agreed to meet with the labor leaders only on condition that no public announcement be made of the conference.

Since the beginning of the New Deal era, some of the strongest supporters of agricultural improvement legislation have been city congressmen and senators. The "city slickers" supported such programs as rural electrification, conservation and better roads for rural communities. Yet while urban congressmen generally supported legislation to help agriculture, the strongest opponents of social legislation favoring labor were the senators and congressmen from the farm belt, most of whom regularly cast their votes against all progressive reforms. More startling, the voting record of the farm politicians has been equally bad on social legislation designed to benefit agricultural workers.

The narrow representation within the congressional farm area explains the cold-shouldering of all social legislation. The farm bloc represents the few farm families who produce most of the total farm surplus for sale, while the many families who produce little of the surplus have virtually no representation, nor have the many families who produce just enough, or not quite enough, for their own families to live on. The many who produce little and the many who produce just enough to live on are not big business.

The farm bloc has one hard and fast rule: "socialism will destroy you; but it is not socialism to underwrite farm prices. To put a floor under your own profits in the form of a guaranteed annual profit is simply good business." The bloc is tied to the Farm Bureau, a conservative organization with roots in the 1.5 million rich farmers who produce the 85 per cent surplus. The bureau is powerful in states with a high percentage of wealthy farmers.

This situation explains why the farmer-labor train is still uncoupled. The rich farmers are capitalists in both income and outlook. They are capitalists because American agriculture has had its own technological revolution. Hybrid corn, which increased the average yield from fifty bushels to eighty or ninety bushels per acre, made farming big business.

In the days of my youth, you could start out to be a farmer in two ways: marry the farmer's daughter, or scrape up $250 and buy a team and wagon. Today you can't buy even an acre of good farmland with $250, and the daughters of rich farmers are more and more inclined to marry movie stars. Capital investment on some of the larger farms runs to $50,000 on 160 acres, or $450 per acre. In addition, it takes an estimated $15,000 to $18,000 to equip a modern farm with machinery. A young man cannot start out to farm unless he has inherited an unusual credit rating.

The result is that the size of the farm unit continues to increase. In 1930, family farms averaged 175 acres; in 1946, 207 acres; in 1950, 276 acres; in 1959, 320 acres. More food is produced on less land with less effort and more machinery. As the size of the big farms increases, the chance of success for the small family farm decreases. In Indiana alone, there are 25,000 fewer family-owned farms than in 1939, and fewer and fewer young men can expect to own their farms. For the nation as a whole, the number of commercial agricultural units dropped sharply from 5.3 million in 1930 to 3.3 million in 1958.

Another result of the agricultural revolution is intense stratification of the farm society. In my home town of Wakarusa, Indiana, there are 175 Pennsylvania German families who drive shiny new cars, live in fine brick homes and own beautiful, well-stocked farms. They are the top layer of the farming community. They belong to the minority who produces more food with less labor.

Others have a harder time of it. They own the little, one-family farms which include forty acres, two cows, and maybe a couple of mules. These farmers barely make a living. As the land gives out, they start rotating crops or move on to better land. Since the New Deal they have been somewhat, although not appreciably, better off. Many of them have given up ownership and have become tenants on big, prosperous farms. These people, who once owned their land, go on from year to year hoping that someday they will become landowners again.

The remaining group, unproductive and lacking capital, lives not on the margin but under it. This group is largely identified with the South, the land of sharecroppers. In the poorest county in Arkansas (named, ironically, Magnolia) you can see them anywhere along the road—and the sight is unforgettable. This is the country of the underfed, the houses on stilts, the three little Negro children sharing one shoe among them, with their clothes rotting on their backs.

This group is rapidly diminishing. More than 250,000 persons are leaving the farms each year. The sons come to the cities in droves, and it is precisely at this point that the farm situation bears directly on the problems of city life. Walk through the State and Wells Street area in Chicago any afternoon, and you will see the Holiness missions, the pentecostal rural evangelist meeting halls, the brothels and the beerhalls which have become the new social centers for migrant workers. And almost all these ex-farm boys remain migrant in spirit; few of them ever lose their wistful desire to go home and buy a farm.

Thousands of workers from the sub-marginal farm lands stream into the Delco-Remy plant in Muncie, Indiana. The effect on the city is a housing shortage and a rapid development of slums. The effect on the migrants themselves is equally disturbing: their children run wild, and the parents, tied to a strange and exhausting factory routine, become bewildered. Their bewilderment is reminiscent of the Okies of the 1930s who clung to the land where their ancestors were buried, even though the land had turned to sand.

For all farmers, rich and poor, have one thing in common: the psychology of the man who lives close to the soil. On this fundamental level, city is city, and farm is farm, and never the twain shall meet. The farm group is a permanent society based on common experience, deep roots and communal living. The city is, among other things, a port of wanderers, men of one-generation traditions, men who come and leave at will.

Spengler marked the peak between the rise and decline of cultures as the time when urban civilization begins to predominate over rural culture. He noticed that city cultures destroy themselves by their own rootlessness and restlessness. Whether Spengler is right or not, it is indisputable that farmers—unless sorely pressed—rarely create movements of social protest. In 1934, in Minneapolis, the farmers—sorely pressed indeed—joined in a milk strike and poured their milk on the ground in protest against the rock-bottoming of prices. But this was an unusual incident. I tried to convince some of these same farmers later that their protest was no different from that of a worker striking against the declining price of the only thing he owns, his hands. The farmers turned to me in surprise, explaining, "But the milk was *mine*." To a farmer, property—the land he holds—is not a tool. It is part of himself.

From the beginning of time, the farmer or peasant has been basically religious, even a bit mystical. His natural religion has not prevented him from rebelling on occasion, but it has prevented him from becoming a serious worker in any significant movement. During the farm foreclosure sales between 1929 and 1939, farmers got together to help their indigent brothers. At an auction they would buy a manure spreader and give it back to the farmer whose property was being sold. And if the sheriff tried to carry through the foreclosure, they would threaten to hang him, as in the song, from the nearest sour apple tree. They rebelled because the sheriff dared to touch that which was their whole life, their land. But the farmer is incapable of translating his own rebellion into workers' terms because to him it is not merely wrong but unthinkable to strike against nature. When you don't produce, as in a strike, you are violating nature.

Besides the farmer's own individual attitudes, there are other pertinent reasons for his estrangement from the labor movement. The eight thousand farm papers, once independent, are now owned by public utilities and big corporations. "Boilerplate"— syndicated material sent out by the National Association of Manufacturers and the American Economic Foundation—constitutes the majority of editorials printed in small-town papers, many of which are owned by big business. The farmer sends his children to 4-H clubs and his wife to meetings with the county agent or the home demonstrator. The patron saint of the 4-H clubs is the Armour Packing Company, and agricultural extension courses are almost exclusively controlled by the conservative Farm Bureau.

An exception to this reactionary control is the Farmers Union, which has done such good work in the South that its opponents have been driven to stigmatize it as radical. It offers hope that farmers may yet recognize their common interest with labor. This hope has been quickened in recent years as the Farmers Union has rolled up impressive membership gains in the face of mounting farm discontent.

The farmer is an individualist. He is convinced that he works from dawn to dark three hundred sixty-five days a year, even though he actually works hard only about a hundred days.

A favorite propaganda device of the farm bloc is to argue that no self-respecting farmer can possibly understand the principle of the forty-hour week. The claim may well be true.

This is why labor, in wooing the farmers to unite with it in the cause of social progress, is constantly baffled. The New York labor director is as different from the Iowa farmer as the Paris intellectual is from the Normandy peasant. But peasant or farmer, European or American, the tiller of the soil is subjected to the same pressure of tradition: to obey authority as his ancestors did, to till the land dutifully, to worship whatever gods his father worshipped and, above all, never to question the established order. This tradition has been enormously successful in keeping the farmer-labor train uncoupled. Even when farmers leave the land for city jobs, their tradition holds them apart from their industrial brothers.

The farmer feels free. More often than not, he views the unions as threatening him with regimentation. He sees his freedom as resting on the preservation of his own isolation and of the status quo.

Short of a cataclysmic depression, there seems little hope of overcoming this illusion of separateness. But there is some hope. Consumers are laboring men and women, and their wages make the farmer's sales possible. If farmers can be shown the elementary fact that when wages drop, consumers cease to have purchasing power to buy farm products, they might cooperate with the unions' drive to keep the wage level high.

The challenge is to get the fact across to the American farm public. Union education programs would help greatly. As Lyle Cooper suggested, the best propaganda is personal exposure to the facts. Certainly no opportunity should be lost to make real unionists out of the farmer youths who work part-time in the factories. An effort must be made to buck the vested interests who control the farmer press. Until the farmer recognizes his natural mate in the industrial worker, the Farmer-Labor train will remain a haunting dream for all men of good will.

17. The Moral Dilemma of Democratic Man

There are two basic facts in American life today: (1) man now has at his disposal the power to commit race suicide through atomic and hydrogen bomb warfare, and (2) the closer America comes to war, the closer we also come to the garrison state.

As in Germany during the rise of Hitler, the Protestant church and the labor movement have been among the first to be attacked by advocates of the garrison state. Senator Joseph McCarthy and men of his silk attacked the Protestant church unsuccessfully. With the labor movement, they had more success: certainly members of the labor movement have been sullied in the eyes of the public.

It is not by accident that Protestant Christianity and the trade-union movement have become allies in the stand against the police state. The labor movement, like Protestantism, is made up of many sects. But all these labor sects were founded upon the same ethical commitment: that people are more important than machines and economic advantage. Moreover, the labor movement, like Protestant Christianity in America, is caught upon the horns of a moral dilemma: it stands for ethical values, and yet it is a living part of a rich America which is preparing relentlessly for war.

There is, of course, a difference between these allies. Most idealistic union leaders have seen their ethical goals as primarily social. The church, on the other hand, has often sought two goals: first the salvation of the individual soul, and, only secondarily, a condition of social well-being.

When dealing with the labor movement, as with Protestantism, one may often put too much value on the variety of sects. But there is also the opposite danger: that everything may be lumped indiscriminately under one label. For example, many people, worried about racketeering in unions, make the mistake of labeling all unionists racketeers.

Certainly there is corruption in the labor movement. Certainly there is racketeering—among the hod-carriers, the longshoremen and Jimmy Hoffa's teamsters. Decent unionists are the first to deplore such diseases within the body of the movement, just as decent Protestants are the first to deplore the fake preacher or the opportunistic layman within their ranks. But such corruption is not typical. Take, for example, the United Automobile Workers—progressive, well-informed, community minded and tumultuously democratic.

The United Mine Workers, for another example, demonstrates a unique kind of unionism. It is set apart because of the different conditions with which miners have had to deal. A miner's life is nine-tenths fear of sudden death and one-tenth backbreaking work. Anyone who has read the accounts of mining disasters, the history of the bloody Pennsylvania coal strikes or the story of terrible Harlan County, Kentucky, has at least an inkling of why the UMW is as it is today. The qualities of the leaders are those of the rank and file: fierce and sullen independence, irascibility, a brooding intensity, pigheadedness, violence and a hard core of unbreakable integrity.

The International Ladies' Garment Workers Union, on the other hand, represents a kind of old-fashioned business unionism which differs noticeably from both the UAW and the UMW. The ILGWU has a unique personality, too—sanguine, flexible, given to quick, intricate political footwork and to moderate planning techniques.

Within the labor movement, then, each sect differs vitally from the others. But while there are incidents of degraded unionism, the larger percentage of the movement is made up of honest, dependable, hard-working men and women.

The labor movement is people. These people have banded together for economic advantage, but I would think it foolish to state that the sole purpose of the labor movement is economic advantage, any more than the sole purpose of the Protestant churches in America is the power they can wield as a lobby. The organizers who, in 1931 and 1932, started working for embryo unions for fifty cents a day plus lunch money were motivated by far more passionate emotions than desire for folding money. And the circuit riders who preached the words of Christ and John Wesley were motivated by far deeper passions than desire for prestige.

The trade-union movement is founded on an ethical problem. Let me illustrate: during the summer of 1954, a metal company in Michigan decided to go out of business. An official of the company was delegated to discuss the liquidation with the members of the CIO union organized in the plant. The Michigan CIO Council took this man's speech down on tape.

The official could hardly control the glee in his voice as he announced that the company would liquidate not only its assets, but also the jobs of workers. It's because of you guys, the official said, that we're going out of business. You've got too many old men puttering around the shop, and you make us keep them on because they've got high seniority. You've given us too much trouble; why, every time one of your guys wakes up on the wrong side of the bed, you gotta strike! Well, this is it, boys. We're pulling out and leaving you high and dry because this company is responsible to its stockholders and not to you!

Union members were faced with a tough dilemma. They could accept company terms which would, in effect, eliminate the union altogether; if they did so, the company promised to delay its closing, thus easing the lay-off period and giving the workers more time to find other jobs. The other alternative open to the workers was to get laid off immediately and to suffer company reprisals, especially unfavorable publicity in state and local newspapers to the effect that it was the union's irresponsibility which caused the company to go out of business.

This situation illustrates the central moral and economic issue in the trade union movement: the workers did not own their own jobs; the company did.

The company official who spoke so bitterly to the Michigan workers may have been talking out of turn, but he represented a fairly large and powerful segment of American management when he emphasized that the company's primary obligation was to its stockholders, not to the workers whom it might temporarily employ. He also represented the kind of natural hostility which exists between the worker in the shop and the supervisor—the foreman, industrial official or time-study man. I call this hostility natural because its dynamics exist outside the structure of either company or union policy. It is a personal feeling which is only indirectly related to union obligations or job duties. It is rooted in the resentment of individual workers who know that, except for certain union guarantees, they could be hired and fired at will. It is rooted in the resentment of supervisors who heartily dislike the fact that they must deal with the subtleties of human inertia and individuality rather than with machines.

The voice of the metal company official betrayed his resentment of human quirks. When a man breaks down beyond repair, you can't just junk him as you would a machine. Like too many of his colleagues, the company official considered workers lazy and indifferent people who, except for the threat of starvation, would refuse to work at all. On the other side of the fence, the worker knows that no matter how affable some foremen may be, their basic job is still to get work out of him, just as the job of the company time-study man is to speed up the workers on whom he holds the watch.

Today it is quite fashionable in academic and church circles to emphasize the friendly rapport version of the management-union relations story. Such people believe that amiable smiles and good will on both sides will solve almost any dispute which might arise. After all, labor and management have everything in common. They want to see the factories kept running, jobs plentiful and goods being produced. There is no reason why they cannot solve their grievances and work together for the common goal.

As a matter of fact, however, no amount of friendly shoulder patting has been able to solve the worker-foreman hostility. The

Puritanical idealization of hard work has no meaning for the factory worker, who is tied, day in and day out, to a routine and fatiguing industrial process. The glory of work may still exist for the man who owns his own grocery store, gas station or farm. But even these men are disappearing. The large chain store, the huge consolidated farm and the corporation have reached further and further into the territory of the small independent businessman and the family farmer. There is no glory for the worker who must tend someone else's machine.

This does not mean that the worker's desire for ownership is dead. I remember Myles Horton of the Highlander Folk School workers' education center telling me how he organized a mill town in North Carolina in 1936. At a certain point in the strike, when all the workers were on the picket line, the rumor went out that scabs were working inside the factory. The workers hated this, and it almost broke up the strike. The workers resented having their jobs taken over by scabs, but they resented even more having their machines taken over. They wanted to go back to the factory to keep those scabs away from their machines. Pride in ownership and pride in skill have been almost extinguished by the industrial system—but not completely.

There are two possible ways to restore pride to the industrial process. One is to organize strong and democratic unions which give the workers in the plants a feeling of community and of solidarity. The logical conclusion to this process is ownership of the factories by both workers as well as management (i.e., a worker can own his own machine). But no responsible union leader will admit such a possibility in America today. Socialization of industry is highly improbable, and, even with socialization, the worker-foreman hatred might continue at a deeper, more covert level.

The second possible solution is the automatic factory, and this alternative is far nearer than most people realize. There is already an automatic Ford factory in Cleveland, Ohio, that is run almost totally without workers. This kind of plant may solve the worker-foreman dilemma because all the employees are foremen or engineers. It also means a revision of the old fundamentalist

Protestant work ethic, an ethic on which most of my generation was reared.

If the process of automation is not aborted, the ancient dream of man—a dream beginning with the first wheel—will be within reach and backbreaking drudgery would be abolished.

Yet as the very moment approaches when man will realize his Utopia, he is threatened with destruction by means of atomic warfare. There are few such overwhelming ironies in all of history. Man cannot decide whether to choose life or death.

Here in America, we have never been able to decide whether to use our vast production plant to create abundance or scarcity. We believe in producing vast quantities of luxury-necessities to be retailed at bargain prices to millions of consumers. We also act as if the best way to avert depression were to wage a war, or at least an armaments race, during which goods become scarce, factories run at top capacity, unemployment almost disappears and everyone lives better.

Labor stands on the principle that because food is a universal need, there is a universal morality demanding the fulfillment of that need. This, I might add, is a unique concept—unique, and indigenously American. No society before the nineteenth century, with the possible exception of the brief-lived tribunals of the French Revolution, ever conceived of such a moral obligation. Very few twentieth-century societies have spelled the obligation out so concretely. Actually, the idea is part of the Christian tradition, for American labor is demanding that the principle *Thou art the keeper of thy workers* be observed in letter and in spirit. As consumers, labor would complete the maxim: . . . *as thy workers are the keepers of thee.*

This, then, is the gist of the matter. Behind demands for better wages, shorter working hours, pensions and other so-called fringe benefits stands one deep and passionate desire: the desire of individual workers to be treated as human beings rather than as mere commodities on the market. The genius of Protestantism has always been its demand that the individual conscience be held in respect. The true aim of the labor movement is the same: that the individual be held in respect, that the industrial system be pre-vented from swallowing him up as if he were a piece of timber or a slab of steel.

Yet labor, like religion, cannot always live by its own ideals. All decent unionists believe people are more important than prop-erty, but like most Americans they must ignore the plight of peo-ple in other areas of the world in order to keep a fairly decent standard of living for themselves.

George Orwell, in an essay on Rudyard Kipling, put the matter this way:

> All left-wing parties in the highly industrialized countries are at bottom a sham, because they make it their business to fight against something which they do not really wish to destroy. They have internationalist aims, and at the same time they struggle to keep a standard of life with which those aims are incompatible. We all live by robbing Asiatic coolies, and those of us who are "enlightened" all maintain that those coolies ought to be set free; but our standard of living, and hence our "enlightenment," de-mands that the robbery shall continue. . . . [Kipling] sees clearly that men can only be highly civilized while other men, inevitably less civilized, are there to guard and feed them.

The labor movement in America, which generally stands a little to the right of the New Deal, is caught squarely on the horns of that moral dilemma. During World War II, the working man made money, or at least more money than he had made for a long time before the war. Many people resented this: between 1941 and 1945, angry letters in the press complained that workers were making plutocratic wages in defense plants while young men were dying overseas.

The people who wrote those angry letters generally forgot that other population groups were also making more money than they had before the war. Executives, in particular, could afford the best night clubs and the best restaurants; many could support at least two homes.

The worker, on the other hand, has never made enough money to be called rich. In the times of greatest economic expansion—war times—he has made enough to live modestly. If he is highly skilled, has a good deal of seniority, and belongs to one of the better unions, he usually has enough money to buy a good solid home, to keep meat on the table, to keep his wife attractively dressed and to buy and maintain a car and a television set.

Usually the worker does not live this well. He may work his head off, save his money, plan for any number of rainy days and still be caught in the maw of an unpredictable economy. The miners in the eastern Kentucky coal fields were getting caught, for example, in the late summer of 1954. We began to see again the old, familiar Depression photographs from that area: the father without prospect of work, the seven children in the three-room jerry-built cabin, the atmosphere of hopeless need.

The worker is always haunted by the fear of sudden poverty, layoffs and debt because no matter how well organized his union is, no matter how hard he works, no matter how many concessions he and his fellows wring from management, he is still at the mercy of an economy which nobody has learned to control.

The other horn of the dilemma is that the organized American worker generally lives at a level which, in comparison with the rest of the world, might be called plutocratic. This is a sin which he shares with most of his fellow Americans, and he feels guilty about it. The American labor movement contributes thousands of dollars a year to the International Confederation of Free Trade Unions, which is responsible for sending money to struggling trade union groups throughout the free world. The progressive elements in the American labor movement have for a long time been internationalist: there are resolutions supporting foreign aid, repudiating the policy of massive retaliation and supporting redevelopment projects in the underdeveloped areas of the world.

Nevertheless, the moral dilemma remains. Many workers in this country would like to feel that they support their working brothers in Europe, South America and Asia, but they cannot. For in principle they support the idea of nationalistic war. They use war to gain wage increases, and they use arms races to perpetuate their economic gains. Indeed, there has never even been a successful international working men's movement which opposed war. Even the most sustained and enthusiastic attempt at a labor pacificist movement, organized under the socialist auspices just before World War I, collapsed miserably when the war actually broke out, and its German leaders were brutally murdered by other workers.

Nevertheless, I do not see how any Protestant Christian can criticize the labor movement for its defection in this area. Churches go promptly nationalist at the outbreak of every war. All over the world pastors pray fervently that their own sides will win. And can we really say that today, in the cold war, we have a world-wide movement of churches striving for peace?

The dilemma is essentially the same as it has always been: "Render unto Caesar the things that are Caesar's"—but what things are they? Can we sanction the use of the hydrogen bomb and still retain our self-respect? Where is the point beyond which no compromise with Caesar is possible?

18. Peace, Politics and Pragmatism

Among the irreversible changes of character of the past few decades has been the transformation of the labor movement from a primarily economic body into an economic-political pressure group. Since the development is relatively new in this country, many people are confused by it. The confusion is easy to understand. If you had asked the late Philip Murray and the late Bill Green about the American economic system, both men would have stated that their faith in free enterprise was absolute. Yet when negotiations became bitter, they declared that the malefactors of great wealth were standing in the way of economic justice. Championing the cause of noncontributory pensions during a strike, Murray brought the steelworkers to their feet when he cried, "I would like to ask Mr. Moreel, of Jones and Laughlin, if Socialism begins at $50,000!"

Similarly, if you had asked Jack Kroll and James McDevitt, the former heads of the CIO's Political Action Committee and Labor's League for Political Education, what the official policies of their organizations were in regard to political action, they would have replied that they sought to elect labor's friends and defeat its enemies. If you had then asked, "Does this mean that you support Democrats only?" they would have replied emphatically, "Of course not. We support men regardless of party label."

Idealists who criticize labor have often pointed to a lack of basic political or economic philosophy. Labor certainly lacks the dogmatic political or economic faith which takes precedence over the day-to-day tasks its leaders are called upon to perform. But this does not imply that the leaders have no philosophy at all. They do.

I would call the philosophy of labor's leaders pragmatic dynamism—that is, the supreme importance of meeting the day-to-day economic and social problems which affect the workers. Leaders must deal realistically with the fact that workers are activated more by money in their pockets than by the most well-ordered utopian blueprint.

The apparent vacillation of labor's leaders may be accounted for in large part by the voluntarism and pragmatism of the larger American political structure. At the bargaining tables, their efforts are conditioned by the fact that they negotiate within the system which they seek to reform. Similarly, the political leaders must get a job done within a framework of parties which they do not control.

To understand labor's role in politics, it is necessary to realize that the labor movement was born of Gompers and pragmatism. Its conscious interest in politics evolved simultaneously with the depression of the 1930s, the Roosevelt era and the New Deal. The CIO was formed in a period when it had the blessings of government. All the men instrumental in the formation of the CIO-PAC held a firm mental grip on Article 7A of the old National Industrial Recovery Act, which guaranteed

> that employees shall have the right to organize and bargain collectively . . . that no employee . . . shall be required as a condition of employment to join any company union or to refrain from joining, organizing, or assisting a labor organization of his own choosing; and that employers shall comply with the maximum hours of labor, minimum rates of pay, and other conditions of employment, approved or prescribed by the President.

This article was the basis for the Wagner Act. Nor has it been forgotten that Roosevelt virtually insured the success of the formation of the CIO and the passage of long awaited social legislation.

Hillman, Murray and Green had access to the White House throughout the Roosevelt administration. To these men Roosevelt was an artist in the field which was to them the master craft, the manipulation of men. It was natural that their politics should be oriented toward keeping Roosevelt in office, for he was a man with whom they could do business.

In the presidential election year of 1948, the picture began to change. Jack Kroll and Joseph Keenan, labor's political action chairmen, were in that select minority of men who consistently predicted Truman's victory in 1948, even against all apparent odds. The basis of their faith, as nearly as I could determine at the time, was their intimate knowledge of labor's increased activity in ward and precinct politics. This grass-roots approach to politics contrasted markedly with labor's efforts in earlier campaigns, when mass propaganda and pamphleteering received more emphasis than local politicking. Both Kroll and Keenan were practical trade unionists, men with years of organizing experience behind them. In the early days of the PAC, Sidney Hillman had surrounded himself with college-trained men who believed that elections could be won by the manipulation of mass media. Under Kroll and Keenan, education was not neglected, but practical trade unionists put leg work before art work, nose-counting before pamphlet distribution.

Labor's efforts in the latter weeks of the 1948 campaign seem even more amazing when we recall that its top leaders were not particularly enthusiastic about Truman. To most of them, Roosevelt was still the President and Harry Truman a dangerous unpredictable who blew up when the railroad workers went on strike. In fact, top labor leaders and many Roosevelt liberals made successive attempts to draft General Eisenhower to lead the disillusioned and disorganized Democrats to victory. Many of these people believed that General Eisenhower would develop into another Great White Father. They reasoned that he was born on their side of the tracks and that, if elected by the Democratic party with labor's help, he would naturally understand the necessity of dealing with his labor supporters fairly. Eisenhower's refusal to run on the Democratic ticket was a blow to the labor leaders, who accepted Truman's nomination without much enthusiasm.

As a result, labor's strategy in the early summer of 1948 was comparatively simple: emphasize the senatorial and congressional elections, control inflation, wipe out the threat of Taft-Hartley— and if Harry Truman should be accidentally elected as a by-product of these efforts, labor would be agreeably surprised. Only later, when the crowds coming out to Truman's whistle stop grew larger, did the attitude of labor's political leaders change and their support for Truman increase.

Labor's emphasis on the senatorial and congressional elections stimulated local political activity. Victory at the polls became increasingly dependent not only on the individual American voters who make up their own minds, but also on the political amateurs who are determined to take a hand in the local governments.

Truman's election meant a resurgence of the Democratic party and ended any immediate plans for a labor party. Labor could still express itself through top levels of the majority party, a party which included many liberals from the ranks of the white collar workers and the farmers, who would not feel at home in a labor party. For better or for worse, labor married itself to the Democratic party.

The 1952 election revealed that the labor politicians had not developed a strong enough grass-roots organization to carry through on their 1948 victories. It also revealed that the wives and sisters of union men are far more important than most union men will admit. A large percentage of these union women bolted to the Republicans in 1952, displeased with their minor status in the union organizational structure and lured by the Eisenhower slogan, "Let's clean up this mess."

But one of the main results of the 1952 election was to emphasize the fact that men on both sides of the Labor-Democratic liaison considered the match nothing more than a shotgun wedding. Labor has never decided how far it intends to go in taking over or in being taken over by the Democratic party. The Dixie-crats, for instance, consider labor infiltration a direct and unholy threat.

In order to be effective within the Democratic party, labor

must find its place in state and city machines. It must become a
part of every state and city central committee, every ward and
precinct organization. Labor must have a voice in the selection
of candidates who run for office. Otherwise, the American public
will hold the labor lobby responsible for exercising political power
which it does not have.

This Labor-Democratic relationship can take several forms.
First, labor can move in on the party organization and administer
it directly or through sympathetic persons. Secondly, it can develop a *modus operandi* by which it bargains with the Democrats
on program, candidates and the operation of elections. The third
possibility, which I think most feasible, is the gradual absorption
by labor of the Democratic machinery and the control of its organization.

The drawback to such avowed control of the party organization would be the public knowledge that labor, in so many places
a minority, had control of a local political party. Whenever this
has happened—as in Ohio—labor has become isolated, and opportunity for alliances with other groups has been lost. There
may, therefore, be some argument for keeping labor in the background and mobilizing its forces quietly.

I do not think that a labor party, as such, is feasible today.
Except in a few large industrial cities, labor cannot win an election alone, certainly not while its members vote as independently
as they did in the 1952 and 1956 campaigns. As Walter Reuther
stated ruefully, "Nobody can deliver the labor vote."

However, if organized labor wishes to be successful in the
future, it must gain more than a voice in the selection of candidates. It must develop its own candidates. At the grass-roots
level, organized labor should encourage its ablest people to seek
positions not only in local governments, but in private civic bodies,
such as the boards of trustees of educational institutions. Candidates do not spring full-blown: they must be nurtured and groomed
to maturity.

But after grooming its candidates—and financing them,
rather than forcing them to mortgage their homes to run for pub-

lic office—labor faces an even larger problem: the problem of shaping a program. The pragmatic dynamists most frequently fail on the programmatic level, and in most elections, labor takes a position of protest.

It is, of course, precisely at this point that the advocates of a labor party advance their strongest case. They argue that a truly realistic and positive platform can be developed only when labor has a vehicle of its own. The advantages of a labor party—or labor's gradual absorption of the Democratic party and control of its machinery—lie chiefly in the fact that labor would then have a vehicle capable of arousing moral enthusiasm. Many men in the labor movement support this view, but it will be a long time before they prevail. The top officers of the AFL-CIO are much more interested in day-to-day victories in collective bargaining than in developing an educational vehicle that, while strong in theory, may be weak in performance.

A pivotal resolution of this conflict occurred with the election of Walter Reuther to the CIO presidency in 1952. With the election of Reuther, the brickbat era was officially ended and the era of labor facts officially begun. Not that Walter Reuther and his men were any less pragmatic than earlier labor leaders but their pragmatism went armed with statistics rather than clubs.

The brickbat men have always claimed to be the most practical. A young man who headed a state CIO research council told me that every year, when the research men went to ask for money from the national CIO, the older school of pragmatic unionists asked, "Why are we paying for paper work? We need brickbats!"

The brickbat school argues that a union has the right to demand wage increases but not to interfere with the prerogatives of management in selling its goods for what the market will bring. Reuther insisted that "The worker, while deserving the highest possible standard of living, is primarily a part of the community and must strive to eliminate the vicious circle of higher wages being swallowed by still higher prices." When he was fighting for leadership of the UAW against Addes and Thomas in 1947, Reuther declared that "We condemn the discredited policy of the old-line labor leadership which pretends to promote the interests of the workers by conspiring with management . . . to exact higher prices from customers."

The old-timers—the brickbat men and the business unionists—gathered brain trusters about them in the uneasy manner that the *nouveaux riches* collect original paintings. Walter Reuther, on the other hand, brought together the bright young men from government, from the universities and from the technical mills which train economists. He employed them in a businesslike fashion. "We recognize," he stated in 1948, before the Democratic Platform Committee, "that organized labor cannot solve its basic problems inside an economic and social vacuum, and that we shall find solutions to our basic problems of all the people in our society."

19. Labor, Politics and Protestantism

Protestantism is in the same relationship to the labor movement as the farmer is. In the case of the Protestants, however, the bride is hardly so reluctant. There have been tentative overtures on both sides, and a number of bodies have been organized, such as the Religion and Labor Foundation, the Commission on the Church and Economic Life of the National Council of Churches, and the social action commissions of the various denominations to bring the two closer together. But it is hard to say who is courting whom. The situation is complicated by a third party, Protestantism's well-organized rival, the Association of Catholic Trade Unionists, which has already made a successful alliance with labor and which produces a cadre of worker-priests for close liaison with certain powerful segments of the labor movement.

There are good reasons why contemporary Protestantism might join with labor on certain well-defined issues. Rebellious Methodism influenced the development of trade unions in England. An English friend once explained why labor unions in his country had not gone either communist or fascist. They were constrained by the influence of the chapel, the co-op movement and the Methodist lay preacher. Similarly, in the thirties, dozens of CIO organizers in the South were former ministers who, having seen the horrors of the Depression, threw off their clerical robes, joined the labor movement and went out to preach to the workers. Biblical rhetoric provided many of these men with a vocabulary which seemed radical even to the young and zealous labor pioneers.

Today, the Protestant church and the labor movement are in somewhat analogous stages of development. The lay preacher doesn't ride any more, and the missionary organizer of 1937 now has bureaucratic powers and a well-defined organizational role. Both church and labor have become conservators of previous gains rather than pioneers in new fields. Both are worried about membership rolls and dues-paying membership. And both groups, of course, presuppose a moral basis for their activities. But neither, as I once wrote, sing any more, or testify or pass out literature.

While I was Director of Research and Education for the CIO, Brethren and other Protestant leaders came to me seeking labor's help on legislative issues. They were concerned about militarism in America. Generally, they agreed with the CIO, which was also antimilitary. When the positions did not meet, however, I suggested that more might be accomplished if church representatives became interested and helpful on labor issues, such as repeal of the poll tax, national FEPC, a minimum wage and social security.

My hope in suggesting this was that a working relationship might be established between the church and labor in which *quid pro quo* would be taken for granted. Such a relationship was not, however, easily achieved. The main reason for the difficulty was that neither Protestantism as a whole nor any denomination within Protestantism could present a well-defined political strategy.

The Protestant leaders with whom we dealt seemed unable to accept the fact that they were living in a period of revolution. They saw revolution in terms of the Russian Communist revolution, forgetting the technological revolution taking place in the United States.

Further, most Protestant leaders have forgotten that there have been other occasions in history when diametrically opposed world outlooks struggled for hegemony. Contemporary Russia is not the first absolutism to challenge men. Let us not forget the historical impact of Islam and its conflicts with Christianity, or the fact that the young American republic found it necessary to live in the same world with European absolutisms.

If we have not forgotten these crises, and if we are not too blinded by fear and hatred of Soviet Russia, we may also recall that these political and cultural opposites eventually learned to live together in the same world and contributed much to each other's cultural advance. Had the extremists in either the Islamic or Christian camp triumphed, the liquidation of the enemy would have been more thorough. Balance of power, internal dissensions and a thousand miscellaneous factors finally forced the Moslems to retire to their part of the world and the Christians, willingly or unwillingly, to theirs. In any case, neither the Moslems nor the Christians had access to the weapons of mass destruction which are now ours—all ours.

Our American revolution is changing the world far beyond our comprehension. Most of us can only glimpse the externals: an increase in the multiplicity of gadgets, a future of geometrically progressing material growth. The vague, materialistic faith built upon this gadgetry is that, given enough economic security, the world will achieve political stability. It is not often mentioned by the believers in progressive materialism, however, that the world has not yet recovered from the effects of the first stage of the industrial revolution, which began two hundred years ago. The economic and political ache occasioned by the invention of the first machine is still painful.

With some oversimplification, it can be said that while our technological revolution lacks a dynamic social philosophy, the communist revolution lacks—temporarily at least—a dynamic technology. The Chinese Communists are facing this problem. The Kuomintang has fallen, the ideology has conquered, and the Chinese need machine tools to bring the benefits of the industrial revolution to the masses. America is, of course, the nation with the surplus of machine tools. And America refuses to sell them to the Communists. The Chinese Communists are taking the long road toward efficient technology by themselves.

Their dilemma poses a reverse problem for us. Our efforts to further the economic recovery of war-torn nations were meant to help them resist communist blandishments. But a strengthened economy, we found, was not enough; so now we are moving to strengthen these nations militarily as well. This invariably means weakening our ties with the people. We are strong in money and guns, weak in ideology, lacking in a positive program of democratic, economic and political organization. We have allied ourselves with reaction in China, Formosa, Latin America, Portugal, Spain. The peoples of the world distrust us, for they have seen us endorse Syngman Rhee, Batista, Peron, Franco, Chiang Kaishek, the United Fruit Company—every reactionary, indeed, except Communist Russia.

An intelligent Protestant strategy would take these things into consideration. But such a strategy would be dependent on the establishment of a politically conscious church, a church willing to abandon its aloofness in order to reclaim its efficacy as an agent of moral stimulation and social responsibility. And this kind of witness is impossible without conversation with those parts of humanity labeled communist.

As a member of the Department of the Church and Economic Life of the National Council of Churches of Christ in America, I noticed that all of us worked hard, wrote our reports and ultimately had them adopted. I noticed, too, that nothing happened. Almost every meeting was devoted to contrasting Catholic political potency with Protestant impotence, and there was more than a little envy in our hearts. Some in our midst felt that the way to potency lay through a more monolithic church structure, so that Protestants might speak with one voice. They would ally us with big labor, big business and big government.

I reject this position. However, the opposite extreme—a situation in which I would have to get in touch with the headquarters of the Brethren church before making a policy decision—would be equally repugnant to me.

I prefer a church which creates a spiritual climate of participation in society so intense that men of ability and integrity are compelled, by the force of their personal ethic, to take part in politics on all levels. The creation of such a climate is not an easy task, for we Protestants are much too inclined to believe that politics and politicians are universally corrupt; and I insist that this climate can only be produced by men and women who live with their fellow human beings; we have no right to preach unless we share.

We offer parts of our lifetime to the state, but not to the body politic. We vote—at least, some of us do—we pay taxes, and we leave the actual administration of politics and government to the politicians. We have forgotten that politics is the art of citizenship, the science of government, the means by which a free society operates. Politics is a natural phenomenon indigenous to every human institution, and the politician acts as a catalyst, bringing about the compromises without which our organizations would be torn apart. Politicians exist in the home, the church, the union and the university, as well as in government. They need to be encouraged rather than scorned.

When Protestants become politically conscious they are inclined to want all or nothing. They become inflexible reformers who scorn compromise. They forget that all dictators begin as reformers.

I often saw middle-class Protestants or their ministerial representatives lobbying in Washington for their special interests. Many times I heard them speak contemptuously of the men they lobbied, particularly if these men were not reacting favorably to the church-inspired pressures. In my opinion, men who refuse to take part in local politics or to encourage others to do so have no right to feel disappointed when they lobby the less friendly representatives elected as a result of their default.

More conscientious Brethren and other Protestants should be in Congress, shaping the decisions; fewer Brethren and other Protestants should be operating through churches as pressure groups. Unfortunately, more and more people are members of special interest groups who demand that their representatives serve their particular interests rather than the public good. As representatives, however, they would discover that with power goes responsibility, and with responsibility goes political accountability to all their constituents.

It is more important for Protestant leaders to keep the people at home informed about legislative issues which affect them than to lobby and pull political wires. This is a difficult task because too many people have lost interest in such issues. Union men and politicians go unrecognized and unsupported by a congregation which feels incapable of influencing the decisions which affect it and which realizes how deeply it can be deceived by the mass media which should inform it.

To overcome such inertia, I think that Protestants should develop and support their own information sources. We need a newspaper which will do for all Protestants what the *Christian Science Monitor* does for Christian Scientists. We need a news service with unchallengeable integrity to serve our Protestant papers. Equally important, we must, in every church, establish cells of not more than a dozen people each who will meet to study and debate the public questions which affect their welfare. Above all, we need to study, to discuss, to understand the manipulative mass media—and somehow to escape their deadly impact.

I believe that our democratic institutions have their origins in the Protestant revolution which insisted on freedom of association, freedom of worship and freedom of political expression. We Protestants are obligated to protect the right of free association and the civil liberties which are the base of our political structure. We must be the instinctive enemies of every demagogue who would make America totalitarian in the name of anti-totalitarianism.

Inevitably, such a strategy demands an unceasing interest in peace and world government. Peace is a necessity in a world already disordered, perhaps beyond repair, and those who believe that wars are inevitable are false prophets.

Karl Barth argues along purely orthodox theological lines that the church commits a fallacy when it takes sides with any state-system at war with any other. (He excepted Nazi Germany because it showed no trace of reason and almost no evidence of law, divine or man-made.) I would agree with Barth because I know that any church which does tie its philosophy directly to the changing fortunes of national states becomes hypocritical and sterile.

The kind of Protestant political strategy I envisage does not mean that the church would throw all its energies into support of the state. This is how the church operates today. The Rotarian middle-class core of American Protestantism has given its support, both covert and open, to the status quo. The state, which is generally accepted as amoral, is thus reinforced by the moral authority of the church. The young, the searching, the vital, the honest—those who are most sensitive to the institutionalization of religion and to the moral rationalization of amoral concepts—increasingly turn their backs on the church.

An economy tied to war, dangerous as it is, is not the most serious threat to free institutions. The ascendancy of the military to the control of foreign policy decisions is even more dangerous, as Eisenhower warned. Worse still is the implied acceptance of the war economy, the trend toward a garrison state and the military ethic by the leaders of communities, labor unions and churches. Decisions which affect the lives of all of us are arrived at secretly, and congressional debate on such issues is so limited that a wider national discussion and understanding of them is almost impossible. The compliance of the churches is also significant. Hitler made a bid for the support of the church and succeeded in getting at least the tacit support of silence.

I speak here, of course, as a son of the persecuted Protestant minorities who fought for the right of free association, the right of individuals to protest and to join others in protest. As a son of that tradition, I say that democracy does not long survive the loss of free association, open caucus and right of protest. It is possible for unions and churches, as for nations, to become totalitarian in the name of anti-totalitarianism. In time of war or threat of war, it is more than possible for a military elite to join hands with labor and the church in a dictatorial, conformist and war-minded alliance against dictatorships, conformity and war. Such a liaison would debilitate the real moral power of both the church and the labor movement.

Protestantism needs a positive democratic faith and program, a conviction that ideas cannot be conquered by force and an awareness of the ascendency of the military in America and what that ascendency means. It must understand the significance of a domestic economy tied to defense expenditures. It must challenge the tendency to accept war—even preventive war—as a solution to our international problems and the tendency in the labor movement to develop a monolithic power structure in defiance of the basic tenets of the democratic faith.

If the church does not begin to understand and face these events, it will indeed become a "perfumed corpse," as George Orwell predicted in his farewell critique of Christian liberalism. And the labor movement, faced with essentially the same dilemma —respectability versus the continuation of its historical role of nonconformity—may also become an institutionalized corpse, embalmed by bureaucrats.

If labor needs the church, the church also needs labor. Certainly, labor is far more respectable now than in the thirties, when the emissaries of the Catholic church first gave their blessing to workers' organization in America. Certainly, the Protestant church in America yearns to reach the workers. Before it can, however, it must face the question of its participation in politics squarely.

Protestantism today has forgotten the meaning of citizenship, as the Athenians knew it. An Athenian took a personal interest in government and judicial business, which we leave to the politicians, whom we so thoroughly despise. He believed that his religion, his games, his marriage, his work, his art, his military service were all aspects of his citizenship. Plato gives us Socrates' definition: "The origin of a city . . . is, in my opinion, due to the fact that no one of us is sufficient for himself, but each is in need of many things. Or do you think there is any other cause for the founding of cities?"

Epilogue: Invocation for a Meeting of Brethren Ministers

We meet today in the potential glare of the hydrogen bomb. We may see more clearly by it; we may be blinded by it. History will judge us.

The hydrogen bomb is the ultimate accomplishment of a civilization that has professed Christianity.

Out of Christian Russia came Bolshevism and the Communist state. Out of Christian Italy came Mussolini and the Fascist state. Out of Christian Germany came Hitler and the Nazi state. Out of the Christian United States came Hiroshima. This after nineteen hundred and sixty years.

Need I recall His sermons now?

The hydrogen bomb exposes our assumption, however much we may deny it, that those who do not believe cannot be brought into belief and therefore must be destroyed before they destroy us, though we may allow them to strike the first blow. Then do not turn the other cheek: drop the bomb! Over the Voice of America preach Christianity; but support gunboats, not missionaries. This after nineteen hundred and sixty years.

Has America become a more Christian nation since the early days of the Republic, since Jeffersonian equalitarianism? We want a sense of history. But what are the trends?

In business: the decline of the small entrepreneur, the proliferation of the corporate giants, the denial of any concept of social justice which suggests a compromise of the principle of profit.

In labor: the decline of the local union, the proliferation of the giant international, the rise of a massive monolithic power structure, the denial of any concept of loyal opposition which suggests a compromise of personal power and immediate political success.

137

In government: the political machine, the proliferation of lobbying and the deal, the decline of the decision-making function of the lower echelons and the non-office-holding citizen, and the introduction of fear—the fear of attending the wrong meeting, saying the wrong word, having the wrong friends, seeing the wrong people.

These are the trends after nineteen hundred and sixty years. What, Brethren, of the churches and the ministers of God? How do we stand in the trends after nineteen hundred and sixty years?

We organize, we lobby, we pass resolutions, we preach, we reason, we argue, we persuade, we write, we publish, we advertise—and then we get the hydrogen bomb. Perhaps we are doing something wrong. Perhaps we are not doing enough of something right.

We have become infatuated with success.

We success-blinded ministers prefer great dues-paying organizations of hypocrites over small groups that have preserved their integrity. A new church is more important to us than a new believer. Our highest faith is placed in lecture engagements, magazine articles and a higher salary.

We have accepted the Coca Cola concept of religion. We produce an effervescent, scintillating, sparkling sermon, attractively bottled in pseudo-psychological terminology, pleasing to the consumer even when it produces spiritual hiccups, and available to all customers at the standardized rate of the weekly contribution. Every Sunday on the pulpit: the pause that refreshes.

Suppose we ministers here assembled were to return to our pulpits, and with us, ministers throughout the land, and were to say to our congregations: We renounce success! And then demand, as Jesus Christ demanded, that the money-lenders leave our temples—and name the names.

Suppose we could abandon the strategies of getting along with the congregations, of placating the pillars of the church, of providing spectator recreation each weekend—and invited those who did not wish to worship to leave. Who would leave and who would stay? What new faces would appear in the pews?

Jesus Christ did not fear to name names. In time long past, even the duke of the city did penance in his shirt-sleeves on the bare steps of the cathedral. Only the salesman must feel assured that all his customers are really good fellows who will name no names, nor call one's sins to one's face.

Have a sparkling sermon or resolution, with that always fresh flavor!

Better yet, suppose we were to leave our churches, so big, so imposing, so heavily insured, and go out among the people. Jesus Christ walked among the people and spoke the words of peace and brotherhood to any who would listen. Suppose we did that. Just imagine doing that! Tomorrow, thousands of ministers leaving their churches, their conferences, their lecture engagements, their studies, their provisions for religious recreation, their concerns for salaries and status—to walk among their fellow men with the words of peace and brotherhood. Imagine thousands of us walking day by day among our fellow men, speaking to all who will listen of the word of God and its meaning for the world today. Who can estimate the consequences? How many would listen, and how many would turn aside, and how many would listen who had never listened before?

Foolish? Is it any more foolish than to do again what we have done before, day after day and year after year, that which has failed to prevent one war, one materialistic revolution, one riot of ugly hate, one atom bomb?

Unrealistic? Is it more unrealistic than going through the same motions we have gone through again and again and again, by which we have earned our daily bread—but not, we can be sure, our eternal salvation?

It would not succeed? Good! Let us fail! Are we succeeding now? Can one more set of resolutions and one more meeting with the big brass succeed where all other conferences, meetings and resolutions have failed? Aren't we heading into defeat at breakneck speed? Could we go down to defeat any faster than by the hydrogen bomb?

Why this worry about defeat? If the divine spark is in man, his quest for God will not end with our poor failure.

Let us not deceive ourselves longer. We are rushing down-hill to defeat. If there is even yet some chance of victory for the brotherhood of man in our time and our civilization, it will not be won by the old ways, the ways of men who did not possess the final weapon, the ways of the big brass making policy; nor will the chance of victory for brotherhood be won by the salesman willing to say anything that must be said, in any way that it must be said, to close the deal, not to lose the sale. If there is a chance for this generation, it lies with those who will meet the absolute weapon with an absolute ethic.

And if there is no chance of victory, then let us go to defeat on our own terms. There is some Christian dignity in that.

I cannot lose that vision of thousands of ministers declaring the words of God in certain and precise terms, naming names, re-lating the classic generalities to the concrete behavior of every man in the congregation: thousands of ministers walking among their fellow men and talking with all as brother and man of God, day after day, all over America.

And if we really did? If we abandoned our conferences and our high-level politics and our big-time lectures and our capital investments and went our way among the people as brothers and men of God? Then might we find the divine spark in our own time? Might we uncover the hidden longing for brotherhood, for peace, for God?

Might we not find followers, hundreds then thousands, our brothers and fellow men?

What then, if we touched the chord that set the chorus? If we uttered the word that started the prayer? All the longing of the people, all that profound yearning of the children of God— waiting to be set in motion. The spark. The spark. The divine spark. What if we dared?

Index

Addes, 69, 127
AFL, 44, 46, 49, 74, 80, 93, 99, 103, 107
AFL-CIO, 52, 90, 127
AFL Teachers union, 12
Agriculture, 77, 82-83, 96-97, 105, 107-8
Alger, Horatio, 47-48
Amalgamated Clothing Workers, 52-53
American Economic Foundation, 111
Anglo-Saxon(s), 6, 27
Armour Packing Company, 111
Art, 2, 35-36, 43, 76, 81, 136
Association of Catholic Trade Unionists, 129
Atomic bomb, 113
Authoritarianism, 23, 56-57, 66
Automation, 118

Barth, Karl, 134
Beck, David, 13
Bennett, Harry, 7, 61
Bias, 5-9, 83, 90, 99
Bible, 14, 20, 28, 129
Brethren, ix, 1-3, 5, 10, 12, 16-17, 19-20, 133; church, 132; communities, 60; educator, 22-23; ministers, 22, 137-40; schools, 25
Brophy, John, 94
Brotherhood, 44, 67, 139-40
Brüderhof, 60
Buber, Martin, 60
Bureau of Labor Statistics, 75, 77, 99-100
Bureau of the Census, 77
Bureaucracy, 11, 46, 49-55, 59, 68, 75, 89, 130, 136

Caesar, 22, 121
Capital, 97, 108-9, 140

Capitalism, xii-xiii, 59, 108
Carey, James, 54, 57-58, 62, 89
Catholics, 28, 60, 132, 136
Censorship, 59
Chicago Teachers Union, ix-x, 49, 61, 74, 78-79, 90, 93
China, 101, 132
Christ, 23-25, 38, 115, 132, 138-39
Christian Scientists, 134
Christianity, 24, 46, 66, 113, 121, 130-31, 137
Christians, 118, 131, 140
Churches, 14-16, 22, 25, 66-67, 113, 115-116, 121; and labor, 129-36
CIO, ix-x, 2, 7, 33, 40, 43, 48-49, 57-58, 62, 68, 74, 78-80, 84, 88-91, 94, 99, 102-4, 122-23, 127, 130; conventions, 39, 63; organizations, 40, 54, 62; organizers, 107, 115, 129; salaries, 54, 62
CIO-PAC, 102-3, 123
Citizens Political Action Committee, 104
Citizenship, 65-66, 72, 133, 136
Civics, 65
Civil liberties, 134
Civil War (Spanish), 2
Civilization, 27, 110, 137, 140
Class structure, 44
Collectivism, 60
Colonialism, 56
Commission for the Reorganization of Education, xi
Commission on Church and Economic Life, 82, 129
Communication, channels of, 61
Communion, 38, 44
Communism, xiii, 24, 37, 59, 82, 90, 105
Communist party, 58
Communists, 14, 20, 34, 37, 69, 86, 129, 132; Chinese, 131

Communitarianism, 60-62
Community, 44, 47-49, 60, 67, 69, 71, 117, 127, 135
Compromise, 14, 25, 29, 66, 71, 75, 81, 83-85, 133, 137
Conformity, 10-11, 23, 135
Congress, 51, 84, 96-98, 105, 133, 135
Conscience, 37, 85, 118
Consumers, 84, 96, 99, 112, 118, 138
Convention Report and Resolutions, 89
Cooper, Lyle, 106-7, 112
Cooperative: farm system, 34; society, xi-xii
Cooperatives, xii, 60, 82
Corporation, 44, 52, 57, 64, 75, 82-83, 85-86, 96, 111, 117; lawyer, 50
Council of Economic Advisers, 84, 96
Culture, 27-29, 31, 67; Far Eastern, 35; rural, 110

Debs, Eugene, 39, 69
Democracy, xii, 23, 29, 32, 55, 61, 66-68, 70-72, 82, 101, 105, 114, 132-36; economic, xiii; political, xiii
Democratic party, xi, 69, 71, 124-25, 127
Democrats, 1-2, 122, 124, 126
Department of the Church and Economic Life, 132
Disarmament, xiii
Dogma, xiii
Dunkard, 16
Dutch (Pennsylvania), 19

Economics, 22, 80, 82-84, 91, 94, 96-97, 99, 104, 106, 114-15, 119, 121
Economists, 50, 73, 75-76, 100, 128
Economy, 84, 120, 131; free enterprise, xi; mixed, xii
Education, xii-xiii, 8, 13, 16, 25, 31, 43, 49, 66, 83, 85, 98; American, 24; political, xi; for sectarians, 22-26; see also under Unions, Workers
Eisenhower, Dwight D., 124-25, 135
Equalitarianism, 137

Ethics, 54, 115; absolute, 140; Brethren, 20; face-to-face, 10; Judeo-Christian, 10, 60, 82; military, 135; personal, 132; Protestant, 118
Evil, 19-20, 22, 31

Factory, 118; Ford automatic, 117; workers, 31-32, 117
Fair Deal, 71
Faith, 1, 66, 122, 135-36, 138
Farm bloc, 108
Farm Bureau, 108, 111
Farmers. See under Labor
Farmers Union, 111
Fascists, 37, 129
Favoritism, 63
FEPC, 130
Fitzpatrick, John, 93
Foreign policy, 90, 120, 135
Free enterprise, 99, 122
Freedom, 13, 112, 134; academic, 25
Freethought, 2

General Motors Corporation, 53
Germany, 134, 137
God, 10, 13, 17, 19-20, 40, 67, 139-40
Gompers, Samuel, 123
Government, 13, 17-18, 45, 52, 60, 71, 84, 86, 97, 99, 101, 128, 133, 136, 138; agencies, 77; favors, 96; local, 126; world, 134
Green, William, 13, 40, 70, 122-23
Guthrie, Woodie, 106

Hamilton, Alexander, 69
Hardie, Kier, 33-34, 39
Harriman, W. Averell, 70
Haywood, Allan, 33-34, 39, 51, 88
Henry, John, 27
Heresy, 23-24, 53
Heroes, 27-32
Hillman, Sidney, 50, 79, 88, 123-24
History, 14, 19, 22-25, 27, 46-47, 51, 87, 89, 93-94, 118, 137; Roman, 56
Hitler, 27, 61, 113, 135, 137
Hoffa, Jimmy, 114
Horton, Myles, 68, 117
House of Representatives, 90
Humanism, 3
Hutchins, Robert, xi, 8, 48

Hydrogen bomb, xiii, 59, 113, 121, 137-39

Idealism, 23, 39, 42, 59, 61, 113
Idealists, xiii, 63, 122
Ideology, 82, 88, 131-32
Imperialism, xiii, 35
Income, 97
Individualism, 10, 57, 60, 111
Institutions, 25, 58, 75, 82, 85, 101, 105, 126, 133-35
Integration, 86
Intellectuals, 37, 81, 94, 112
Intelligence, 6, 62
Intelligentsia, 1, 4, 100
International Federation of Trade Unions, 48, 120
International Ladies' Garment Workers Union, 52, 114
Internationalism, 119-20
Intolerance, 86
Islam, 130-31
Isolationism, 60
Israel, 28, 34

Jefferson, Thomas, 69, 137
Jehovah's Witnesses, 30
Jenner, Senator, 22, 59
Jesus, 12, 22, 24-25, 67, 137-39
Jew(s), 6, 28
Jones and Laughlin, 122
Justice, 101, 122, 137

Keenan, Joseph, 124
Kelly-Nash political machine, x
Knights of Labor, 46
Knowledge, 9, 28, 62, 68, 85
Korea, 35, 51
Kroll, Jack, 70, 122, 124
Kuomintang, 131

Labor, 2, 36, 56, 61, 69, 74, 107, 109, 116, 118; bills, 101; dignity of, 65-66; disputes, 99; and farmers, 106-12, 129; heroes, 46; history, 46, 93-94; ideals, 119; issues, 130; lawyers, 100; leaders, 13, 37, 39-41, 71, 73, 75, 87, 94, 107, 123-25, 127-28; meetings, 46; movement, 13, 43, 47, 49, 71, 73, 75-80, 82, 85, 87-88, 92-93, 100, 102-3, 111, 113-14, 118, 120-23, 127, 129, 135-36; organized, xi,

8-9, 16, 41, 51, 71, 73, 76-77, 82, 87, 89, 92, 96-97, 99-102, 104, 123, 125-26, 128; party, 71, 125-27; and political action, 64-74, 100-1, 104, 122-36; power, 72, 137; press, 91, 98, 105; program, 126-27; and Protestantism, 129-36; relations, 94; world, 50, 78, 80, 94
Labor-Democratic liaison, 125-26
Labor's League for Political Action, 122
Laissez faire, 82
Law, 51, 53, 75, 101; economic, 76
Lawyers. See under Unions
Legislation, xii, 76, 80, 97-100, 107-8, 123, 130, 133
Lenin, 24, 38
Lewis, John L., 39-40, 50, 53, 57, 70, 94
Liberalism, Christian, 136
Liberals, 82, 124-25
Life, 5, 19-20, 25, 28, 31, 65, 76
Lobbyists, 76, 98, 100-101, 115, 126, 133-34, 138
Love, 5, 34-35, 37, 44
Loyalty oaths, 12, 20

MacArthur, General Douglas, xi
McCarthy, Senttor Joseph, 59, 113
McDevitt, James, 122
Man: depersonalization of, 60; dignity of, 14-16, 140; divine spark in, 140; kept, 82-86; and monuments, 8-15, 26; moral dilemma of, 115-21; and need to identify, 58-60, 86; as organization man, 73-81; struggle of, 46; and system, 11-12, 14
Management, xii, 36, 56, 61, 86, 100, 116, 120, 127-28
Marx, Karl, 23, 53, 69
Mass media, 102-3, 124, 134
Materialism, 22, 131, 139
Meany, George, 53
Mencken, H. L., 24
Mennonites, ix, xi, 12, 16, 19-20, 61, 107
Methodism, 129
Michigan CIO Council, 115
Michigan Socialist Party, x
Middle class, 29, 31, 37, 80, 135
Militarism, 130

Mill, John Stuart, 23-24
Ministers, 11-13, 17, 26, 83, 104, 133, 137-40
Monopoly, 32, 106
Morality, 34, 84-85, 118
Morals, 30, 101, 113, 115-21, 127, 130, 132, 135
Murray, Philip, 13, 39-40, 43, 50-51, 57-58, 62, 69-70, 79, 88, 92, 122-23
Music, 36, 38, 43
Mysticism, 110
Myth, 48
Myth-man, 27, 32

National Association of Manufacturers, 111
National Council of Churches of Christ in America, 82, 129, 132
National Industrial Recovery Act, 123
National Reconstruction Act, 99
Nationalism, xiii, 29, 121
Nature, 38, 111
Nazi, 34, 59; Germany, 134
Negotiations, 50, 61, 87, 93, 99, 122-23
Negro, 6, 12, 28, 30, 109
New Deal, 2, 71, 107, 109, 119, 123
Nonconformity, 11, 136

Objectivity, 4-5, 9, 77
Organizations, 133, 138; economic, 83-85, 132; political, 85, 132; see also Labor, Unions
Orwell, George, 119, 136

Pacifism, ix-x, 1, 121
Peace, 22, 122-28, 134, 139-40
Pensions, 32, 50, 53-54, 118, 122
Persecution, 28, 135
Philosophy, 31, 37, 101, 104; economic, 122-23; of history, 89; of reform, 49; social, 131
Pietists, ix, 23
Pinkerton raids, 87
Political Action Committee, 50, 79, 102-3, 122, 124
Politics, 5, 11, 16-17, 23, 29, 34, 36-37, 41, 64-74, 86, 88, 90, 93-94, 98-99, 101, 114, 122-36
Power, 11, 29, 36, 52, 67, 75, 86, 133; administrative, 60; conflicts

of, 78; hierarchy, 54, 64; inner, 37; political, 74, 96, 126; purchasing, 97, 112; structure, 13, 44, 85, 88-89, 136-37; struggles, 34, 38, 91
Pragmatism, 49, 92, 122-28
Prejudice, xiv
President (of the United States), 84, 96, 123
Pressman, Lee, 51, 89
Pressure groups, 29, 85, 97, 101, 122, 133
Price, 96, 99, 101, 105-6, 108, 127-28
Principles, 85, 118
Production, 50, 56, 61, 118
Productivity, 86
Protestant: church, 113, 115, 129, 136; ethic, 118; heritage, 3; impotence, 132; leaders, 130, 133; revolution, 134; thought, 60
Protestantism, 1, 24, 113, 118, 129-36
Protestants, 1, 3, 28, 114, 121, 129, 132-35
Psychoanalysis, 5
Public relations, 75, 102-4
Public schools, 28, 31, 65, 74
Public utilities, 111
Puritanism, 80, 117

Quakers, 23
Questionnaires, 87, 91-93

Racism, 86
Radicalism, ix, 36, 50, 64, 111, 129
Realists, xiii
Retson, 5, 101, 134
Reform, 49-50, 107, 123, 133
Reformation, 24
Religion, 2, 6, 13, 24-25, 28, 33, 110, 119, 135-36, 138
Religion and Labor Foundation, 129
Republican party, xi
Republicans, 1, 125
Research, 49-50, 55, 57, 75, 77-78, 80, 83, 87, 89, 91-94, 106, 127, 130
Reuther, Walter, x, 39-40, 50, 53, 68-69, 126-28
Revolution, 23, 139; agricultural, 108-9; American, 131; Communist, 130-31; French, 118; in-

Index

dustrial, 131; technological, 130-31

Roosevelt, Franklin Delano, 29, 99, 102-3, 123-24

Rotary club, 25, 29-30, 32, 135

Russia. *See* Soviet Union

St. Francis of Assisi, 33, 69

St. Vincent de Paul, 58

Saints, 37, 58

Salary, 139; schedules, 54

Salvation, 113, 139

Schwalm, Monroe, 16-18, 21

Science, 9; of government, 133; social, 4, 8

Scientist, 77; political, 104; social, 4-5

Sectarians, 1-5, 22-26, 53

Secularism, 13, 22

Security, xiii, 46, 50, 53-54, 64, 84, 99-100, 130

Sharecroppers, 109

Silent Generation, 29-30

Slavery, 56-58, 66

Socialism, x, 34, 82, 108, 121-22, 128

Socialists, 2, 69

Socialization, 4, 117

Sociology, 4-5, 53

Socrates, 35, 136

Solidarity, 117

Sovereignty, xiii

Soviet Union, 59, 130, 132, 137

Spinoza, 38

Standard of living, 119, 127

State, 133-34; Communist, 137; Fascist, 137; garrison, 113, 135; Nazi, 137; police, 113

Statisticians, 4, 9, 73, 77, 93, 97, 100, 127

Status, 10, 25, 44, 55, 60, 63, 139

Strikes, x, 36, 40, 48, 64-65, 83, 94, 102, 107, 110, 114-15, 117, 122, 124

Subservience, 57, 104

Symbols, 10, 27, 40

System: economic, 100, 122; industrial, 117, 119; versus man, 11-12, 14; state, 134; two-party, 100

Taft-Hartley Act, 51, 68, 92, 97, 125

Talmud, 28, 30

Teacher and student, 9-10, 12, 14, 24, 30, 87

Teachers Union. *See* Chicago Teachers Union

Theologians, 12, 134

Torah, 17, 28

Totalitarianism, 23

Totalitarians, xii, 134-35

Trade-union. *See* Unions

Truman, Harry, 70, 124-25

Truth, xiii, 9-10, 16, 21, 23, 26, 28, 77, 84-85

UAW, 36, 50, 127

Un-Americanism, 32

Unemployment insurance, 99

Unionism, 33, 44, 114

Unionists, xiii, 112, 114, 119, 124, 128

Unions, xii, 7, 12, 14, 33, 36, 43, 48, 60-61, 86-87, 95, 96-97, 102; administration, 49, 52, 54, 63, 89; careers, 53; and churches, 129-36; conventions, 44, 54, 64, 77-78, 89-91; education, 36, 46, 52, 55, 57, 64, 73, 78, 92, 98, 103, 112, 124, 127, 130; in England, 129; and free world, 120; halls, 13, 47; hierarchy, 90; lawyers, 50-52, 73, 75-76, 92; leaders, 37, 41, 49-50, 64, 66, 70, 76, 79, 92, 103, 113-14, 117; loyalty, 55, 57, 79; members, 47, 51-53, 64-67, 77, 85, 89, 101, 103-4, 115, 125, 130; movement, 13, 49, 52, 91, 113-15; organizations, 40-41, 44, 49-55, 77, 94, 103; policy, 68, 70, 74, 77-78, 83, 88, 116; power, 85-86, 88; practices, 67, 91; programs, 91; racketeering, 114; salaries, 54, 62, 75; secretaries, 43, 54-55, 57, 62-63, 78-79, 90-92; standards, 58

United Automobile Workers, 114

United Fruit Company, 132

United Mine Workers, 114

United Packinghouse Workers of America, 68, 106-7

United States Steel Corporation, 53

Universities, 85-86, 128, 133

University of Chicago, x-xi, 3, 6, 8, 10, 74, 76, 88

Utopianism, 48, 61, 123

Values, 27, 32, 54; ethical, 113; middle-class, 31
Virtue, 28, 30
Voluntarism, 123

Wages, 50, 54, 65, 68, 80, 90, 92, 96, 99, 104-5, 107, 112, 118-20, 127; minimum, 99, 130
Wagner Act, 99, 123
Walsh, Raymond, x, 74, 78-79
War, 5, 22-23, 34, 86, 134, 136, 139; atomic, 113, 118; cold, 121; economy, 135; in Korea, 35, 51; nationalistic, 120
Washington, George, 28-30, 32

White House, 71, 106, 123
Worker-priests, 129
Workers, xii-xiii, 13, 15, 39, 44, 62, 64, 77, 84, 106, 111, 119-20, 123, 128-29; agricultural, 107; automobile, 36, 53, 68, 74, 94; as commodities, 118; education, xii-xiii, 46-48, 68-69, 76, 80, 103, 117; factory, 31-32, 117; jobs, 115-16; migrant, 110; organized, 66, 80, 97; program, 47; railroad, 124; steel, 53, 58, 92, 122; un-organized, 66, 80, 97
World War I, 121
World War II, ix, 61, 119